The Round Houses of 1959 designed by architect James Strutt

Peter D. Geldart

Member, docomomo

The Round Houses of 1959 designed by architect James Strutt

8" x 10"
126 p

Softcover black & white
Hardcover colour

Petra Books
78 George Street, Suite 204
Ottawa ON K1N 5W1 Canada

Front and back cover drawings: G house perspective view and presentation plan. (c) James W. Strutt, 1959.

Partnership stamp and letterheads 1951-1960. Note P.Q.A.A. (Province of Quebec Association of Architects) added by hand (currently l'*Ordre des architectes du Québec*)(c) JWS and associates.

Contents

Preface

This study offers an opportunity to rebuild a Strutt round house (which he had done to then-current standards) with improved insulation and roof support while retaining the mid-20th-century-modern style.

The essential elements — single floor no basement, no garage, and tent-like hyperbolic paraboloid roofs — reduce materials and respect the architect's ideal of a "low-cost house of 1000 sq. ft." The design consists of a central hexagon (kitchen, bathroom, services), surrounded by a curve of bedrooms (two single and one master) and an open living-dining area with two sets of patio windows. Optionally there are two triangular wing rooms and a carport bringing the square footage to about 2000. It is a hexagon within a circle within a triangle under HP roofs.

In keeping with the '50s style, kitchen and bathroom finishing would retain the lemon-yellow arborite with mahogany trim and the 4"x4" yellow tile in the bathrooms. Mahogany panels are used for interior walls and simple "retro" lighting fixtures and door and faucet hardware.

In rebuilding for a Canadian winter there must be improvements to the foundation, structural weight-bearing and insulation. In a temperate climate consideration would be given to the handling of sun, heat and rain.

If built in the Ottawa region this house could be used by a university as a teaching space, as is the case with the first Strutt family house now managed by the Strutt Foundation, or as a residence for architecture students, or some other sustainable model.

The Strutt family must be compensated for use of the original concept and drawings of 1959 by James Strutt.

Please see continuation in the last chapter "Rebuild".

Introduction

James W. Strutt (1924-2008) was an architect in the Ottawa, Canada region practicing as Gilleland & Strutt in the 1950s, remaining active in the field his whole life. He graduated from the University of Toronto in architecture in 1950 and taught at the School of Architecture at Carleton University from 1969, serving as Director in 1987-1988.

Influences included the architect Frank Lloyd Wright and the engineer Buckminster Fuller.

In the '50s a new, hopeful era was beginning. Young men and women were looking to settle down and start families. There was going to be a baby boom, but the generation of free-wheeling youth had not yet arrived. It was now the time to be engaged, optimistic and experimental: a new world was to be created.

"I remember the round houses very well. There was a collective movement of returned veterans and others who, after WWII wanted to create new types of housing based on rejecting the old ways and coming up with new and exciting forms and ideas that were worthy of their new generation. Jimmy's designs represented bold new thinking with a social basis ... Like all Jimmy's houses, economy of materials and construction meant fragility."

-- William Lett, architect
communication with the author, 2023

In 1959 Strutt would gave been 35. This is the year on most of the drawings for the six clients of a "round house" template. No doubt his ideas on the concept preceded client projects, and then when work started he oversaw construction in association with his builder.

Here is his list of "Round Houses & Others" he was in the process of doing in the late '50s.

The truss (a la Buley Fuller) system for the Warnip House Dock.

Strutt at the W house (not a round house, however) with note on the back. c. 1954. (c) JWS

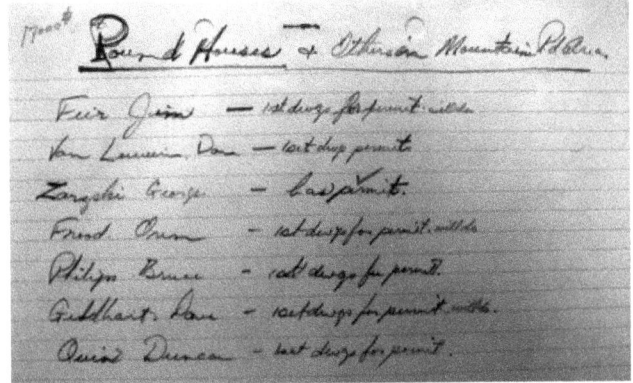

Strutt round houses personal list (c) JWS

Readers can learn more about his legacy at the Strutt Foundation[1] and in the article *The Strutt House* by Hierlihy and Truesdale[2].

1 https://struttfoundation.ca
2 *Heritage & Technology* Heritage Conservation Symposium 2013, School of Canadian Studies, Carleton University) at https://carleton.ca/heritage-conservation-symposium/wp-content/uploads/Hierlihy-CU-HC-Symposium-2013.pdf

1958

NHA

The National Housing Act

A MINIMUM HOUSE

Central Mortgage and Housing Corporation

The purpose of this folder is to describe in brief the specifications of a minimum house that can be built with financial assistance under the terms of the National Housing Act. This house is different from the typical house built for urban dwellers with NHA financing. Most houses built under NHA exceed the minimum standards in a number of ways. To reduce building costs some of these features—such as bathroom, basement and electrical wiring—can be omitted without impairing the soundness of the house. The minimum house is a well-built house which provides all the essentials in space, light, ventilation, materials and construction methods. *It is intended primarily for rural areas where municipal services are not available.*

Where houses exceed or differ from the mini-mum requirements for planning, construction and materials, then these features must at least equal the requirements of the relevant sections of "Housing Standards".

Section 12 (2) of the National Housing Act, 1954, permits Central Mortgage and Housing Corporation to prescribe standards of construction for NHA houses. For this purpose the Corporation has adopted the construction standards of the Division of Building Research of the National Research Council, Ottawa. They are available from any office of the Corporation in a booklet entitled "Housing Standards".

"Housing Standards" details the minimum requirements for planning, construction and materials for NHA purposes *but where municipal by-laws or provincial legislation require higher standards, NHA borrowers are governed by the higher standards.*

The following is an outline specification of a minimum three-bedroom house, without basement, meeting NHA loan requirements:

● SPACE REQUIREMENTS

	Area (inside measurements)	Width
1st Bedroom	110 sq. ft.	9' - 0"
2nd Bedroom	80 "	7' - 0"
3rd Bedroom	80 "	7' - 0"
*Living, Dining and Kitchen	230 "	10' - 0"
Utility	120 "	
Storage	50 "	

* Living, dining and kitchen requirements may be met with an area of 150 square feet with a width of 10' - 0" combined with another area of 80 square feet with a width of 8' - 0". A minimum bathroom, or bathroom space, requires about 35 square feet of area and closets about 27 square feet which would provide for three bedroom closets, one coat closet and one linen closet.

CMHC booklet face 1-2, 1958. Item 1247 https://assets.cmhc-schl.gc.ca/sf/project/archive/publications/pam/pam_cmhc_1247.pdf#page=2

In the Strutt files at the National Archives is a copy of the Canada Mortgage and Housing Corporation leaflet of 1958 entitled "A Minimum House". This government publication may have inspired him to think:

How would I do that?

For the round houses he abandoned the right angled bungalow and based his concept on a curve of rooms and an open living-dining area surrounding the central core of services. This was "informal intimacy" as was said about Frank Lloyd Wright's Pew house[3].

His idea was to reduce building costs by keeping materials to a minimum, yet have an ergonomic, inviting space.

Round house characteristics:

- a single floor with no basement;
- poured concrete foundation slab floating on prepared sand or ground;
- optional carport, no garage;
- lightweight laminated and nailed boards forming a hyperbolic paraboloid (HP) roof, no attic;
- centralized services (heating, plumbing, electrical); and
- an open-concept living-dining area with two sets of full-height windows facing patios.

---

3 Learning to Look, Joshua Taylor, p60, University of Chicago Press, 1957

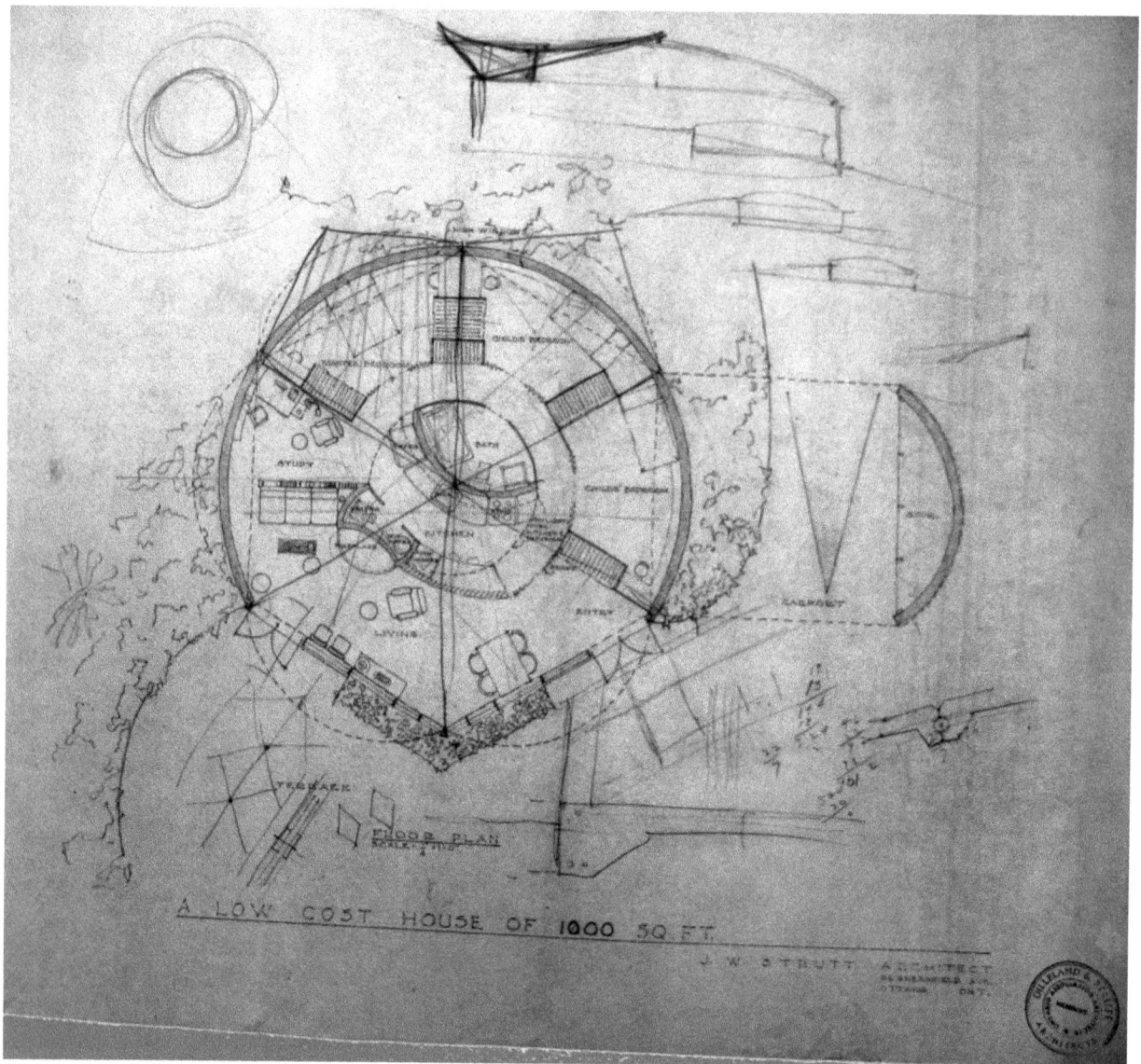

One of the earliest sketches of a round house, "A low cost house of 1000 sq. ft." Carport (right), no wing rooms. Note: "1200" was changed by hand to "1000".(c) JWS

In this drawing there are aspects that are not on other plans in this book: the kitchen-bathroom have a common curved wall, and the central core and hallway have curved walls; it would be a challenge to have wood panels and concrete block walls on that radius, and to connect the HP ceiling to the central core. There are double doors and a moderate-sized window facing the two patios, not extensive patio windows. The carport outside wall follows the curve of the house, but is more concave. Further, he was experimenting with roof overhangs, curved or pointed.

The round houses later developed have a central hexagon tower of 8'-wide sides within a 45' diameter circle with up to three triangular "wing" extensions. In the centre tower is a services room, kitchen and bathroom. A hallway and bedrooms are arranged on one half of the outer curve of the circle and an open living-dining area with two sets of patio windows make up the other half. A triangular-shaped carport and wing rooms are options. Based on my research at the National Archives, Strutt had four types of round houses:

- No wing room, carport only;
- One wing room, with carport;
- Two wing rooms, no carport; and
- Two wing rooms, with carport.

There were no drawings at the National Archives of the other possibility of "One wing room, no carport".

Depending on the characteristics of the lot, and the client's requirements, in some cases the carport would be drive-through and in other cases it would simply be a parking space. In some cases the two sets of patio windows were on opposite sides of the living area and in other cases they abutted each other at an angle in front of the living area.

The fourth type in the list above is the most complete with a carport and two wing rooms[4], forming a large bounding equilateral triangle having approximately 70' sides.

*

I examined what was at the National Archives of Canada where much of Strutt's work is kept: reference R5736 *Series 1: Housing/Single-family Dwellings* and *Series 13: Weight-efficient Buildings*. All drawings are (c) James W. Strutt, or JWS (and associates) and the Strutt Foundation.

---

4 In the G house one was a recreation room and the other an apartment suite with a shower, kitchenette, exterior entrance and double doors to the main house.

The round house concept was a valid and creative attempt to meet the need for single-family homes after WWII. But unlike a bungalow they had a unique beauty with much open space, a sense of proportion and symmetry, with a low profile fitting into the landscape. There is a great sense of freedom of movement with the living-dining area connected in a great circle through the bedrooms hallway. The outdoors is always visible with two sets of full-height windows facing onto patios.

This presentation is largely visual using reproductions of architectural drawings by Strutt (Gilleland and Strutt) with descriptive captions by the author, as well as photographs of an example house showing construction, architectural elements and living circumstances. The architectural drawings are not cast in stone: in at least one house a different concrete block was used than is shown in the plans; one drawing shows a carport whereas another shows a wing room and no carport. These may have been options to be shown to clients.

Is the concept of a "low cost house of 1000 sq. ft." viable in the 21st century? Certainly less material and a reduced footprint are sound principles. While the house was built to the standards of the day, it can now be built using modern materials and techniques.

*

The following table demonstrates that by 1959 he had developed a single-family round house model he could customize for various clients. I have used the first letter of the last name of the client to indicate the houses. Some were planned but not built; some have since been demolished.

Client		Wing rooms	Est. sq ft	Carport parking	Carport drive-through	Patio window walls abutting	Patio window walls opposing
F Frood		2	2000			2	
F variation		1	1700	1		2	
FE Feir			1400	1			2
G Geld[h]art		2	2000		1		2
P Phillips			1400	1			2
P variation		1	1700	1			2
V Van Leeuwen			1400		1		2
Z Zarzycki			1400	1			2
Z variation		1	1700	1		2	

Notes: Estimated useable square footage not including carport. Carports are indicated by an arrow in the house icons. The entrance to the house is usually associated with this area.

Presentations & Plans

In these perspective drawings one can see the draftperson's pleasure in drawing the house and adding landscaping elements. The drawings were used to present options to clients:

- a minimum sq. ft. house plus a carport. The carport is one wing of a hypothetical triangle which encloses the circular floor plan.
- an additional triangular wing room.
- a second triangular wing room which then completes the enclosing triangle. (G house)

Z house variation with parking carport, one wing room, abutting patios. Note privacy walls adjacent to the patios are five x 16" blocks high with an angled end. The height of the short wall in front is one 16" block. (c) JWS

Plans

The geometry of a round house begins with a concrete block hexagon tower of 8'-wide sides at the centre of a circle about 45' in diameter. The structure sits on a floating concrete slab. Optional triangular wing rooms, also on a concrete slab, and/or a carport are added. The span of a wing room, patio and a second wing room is about 70', that is, this is the length of the side of the overall bounding triangle. Thus the full area, not just floor space, based on the circle is about 1600 sq. ft. and based on the triangle is about 2200 sq. ft. (i.e., with a carport and two wing rooms).

Bedrooms including a master bedroom follow the rear curved block wall. On the inner side bedroom doors open to the hallway the roof of which forms an upper "shelf" in the bedrooms. Two sets of full-height patio windows along with one or two doors, face onto terraces. A fireplace in the central core faces the living area.

Centralized Services

There is a core of services in the central six-sided block tower comprising a separate kitchen, bathroom and "furnace room" (heating, electrical, plumbing). Hot air supply ducts fan out from the centre within the concrete slab to the perimeter of the circle where they continue around with periodic supply grills. Return air is passive through openings above the furnace room.

Water supply comes to this central room from the wellhead and copper pipes go to the adjacent kitchen and bathroom; if necessary, pipes lie in the concrete slab to reach a laundry room and apartment suite. A water softener may be installed.

Electrical wiring leaves the main panel in this central room to supply the hot water tank, furnace and the adjacent kitchen and bathroom. For the rest of the house wires lie along the tops of the walls and inner roof eves and within walls to reach electrical sockets and lighting. It is an attractive feature to have recessed lighting in the roof eves, even in the bedrooms, which illuminates the roof boards. Telephone service also enters at the centre and leads, initially, to one outlet near the kitchen.

Waste water piping is embedded through the concrete slab to reach the exterior septic tank and weeping tile bed.

*

In some early concepts of the F and FE houses Strutt drafted straight exterior walls but in the final versions used curved block walls (see following pages).

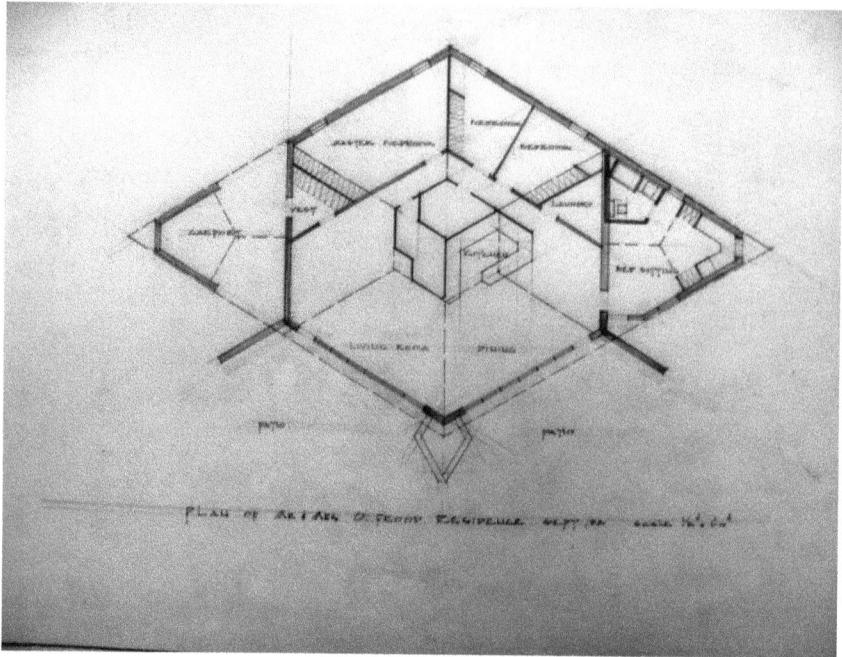

F house early variation with parking carport, one
wing room. Note abutting patios. The diamond shape
and the straight bedroom walls were later drafted as
curved walls (see following F house drawings).
(c) JWS 1958

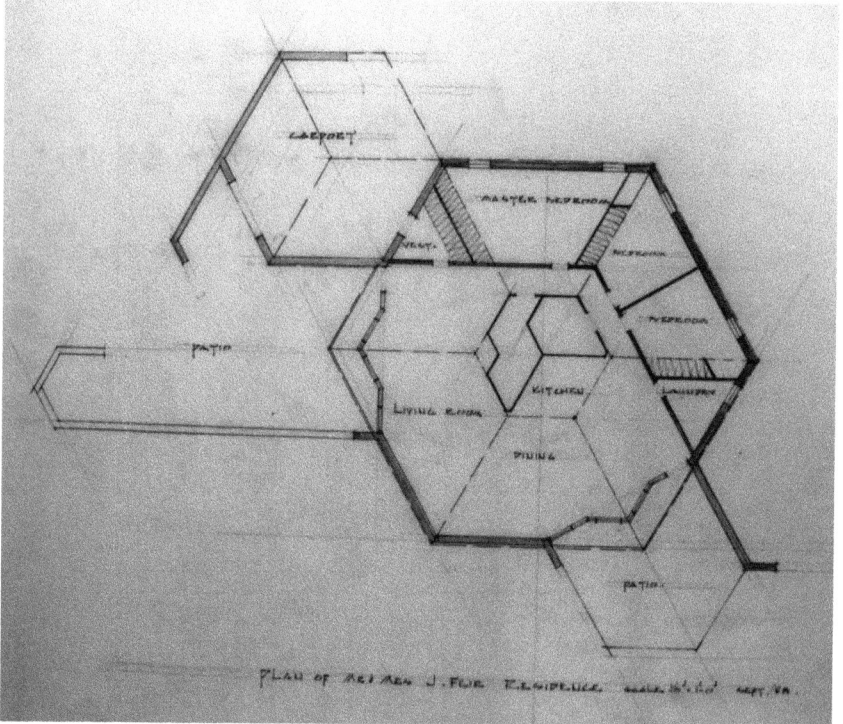

FE house early presentation plan. Parking carport,
no wing rooms. The straight walls belie the future
curved exterior walls (see following FE house
drawings). Note angled patio windows. (c) JWS 1958

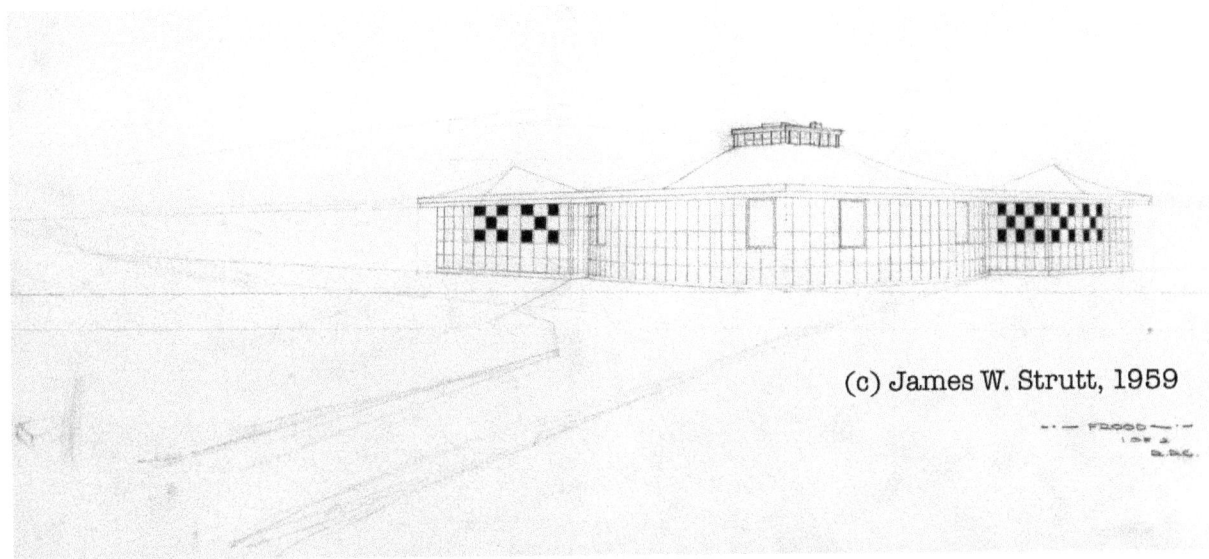

F house rear elevation with bedroom windows on curved wall. (c) JWS

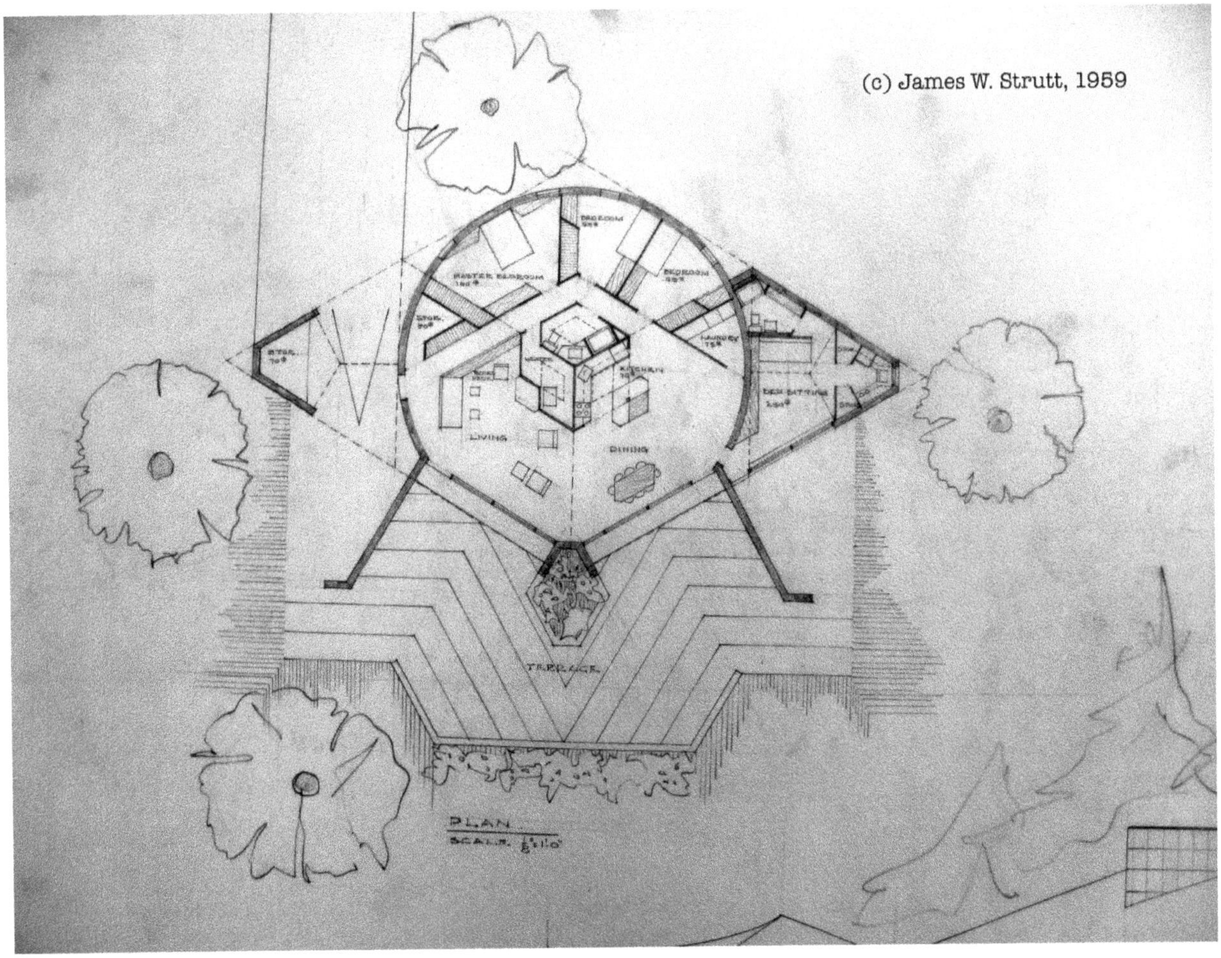

F house presentation plan. Abutting patios. (c) JWS

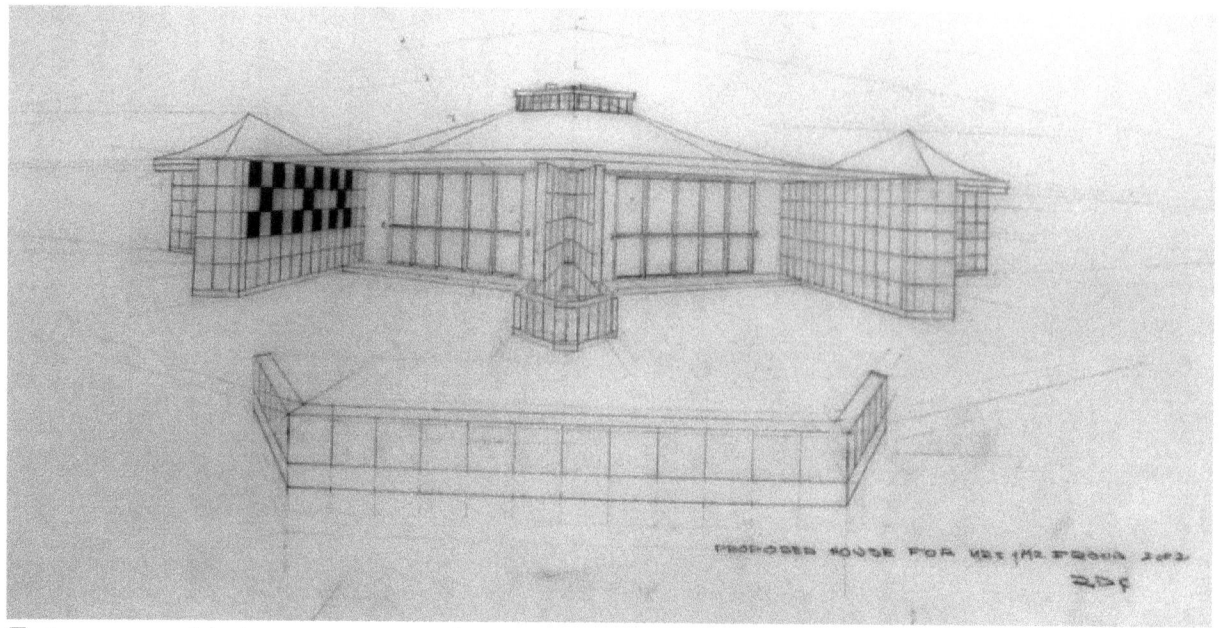

F house preliminary perspective, front view. Note abutting patios and glass block pattern on the privacy wall (left). 2 of 2. (c) JWS

F house rear view showing bedroom windows on a curved block wall. Two wing rooms, no carport. Note patterns of glass block "windows". (c) JWS

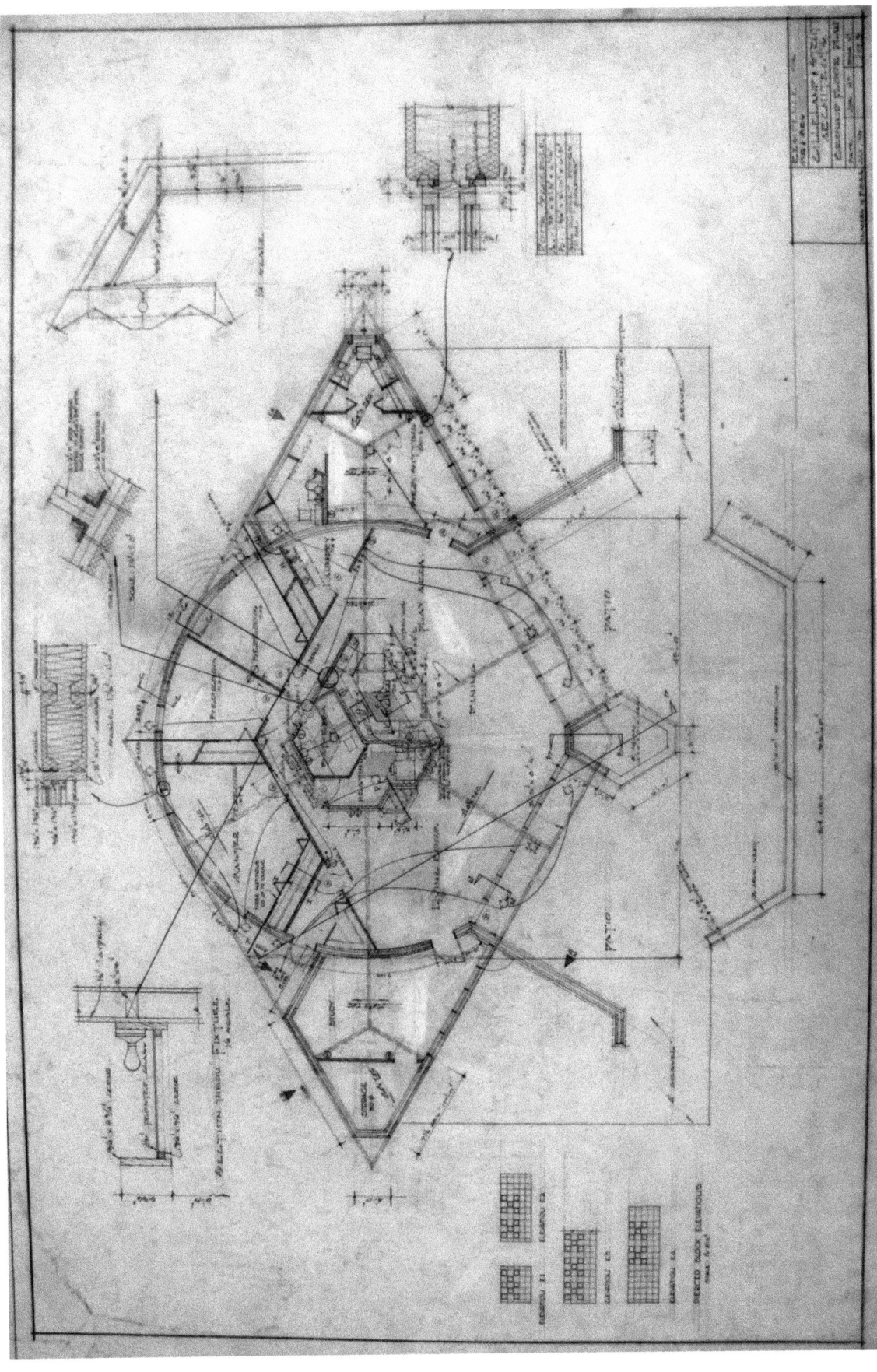

F house. Two wing rooms with entrance vestibule (left). No carport. Note abutting patio windows and adjacent privacy walls (five x 16" high) with an angled end; wall in front is one x 16". Note "pierced block elevations" lower left, i.e. glass blocks replaced concrete blocks. (c) JWS

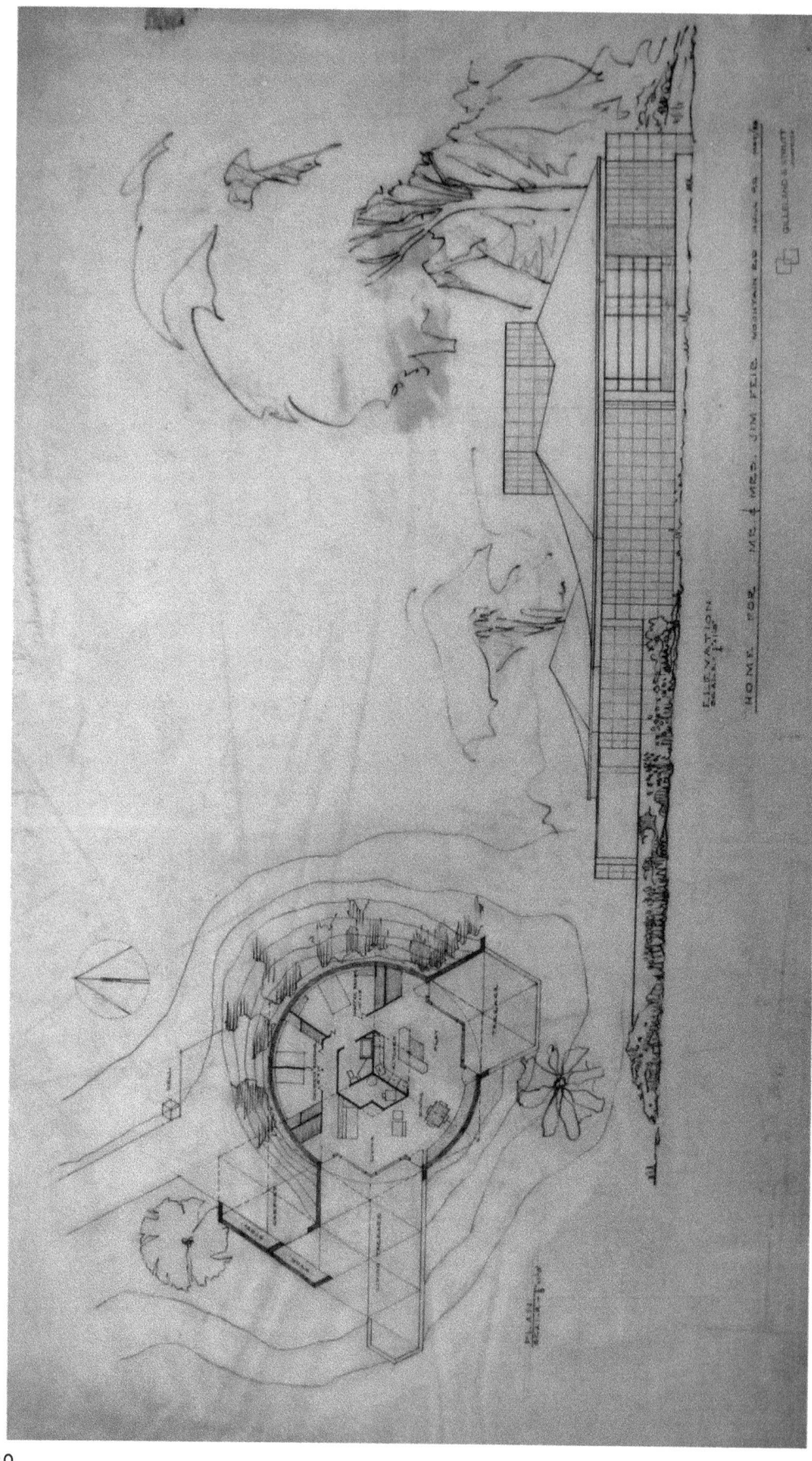

FE house with parking carport, no wing rooms. Note curved block walls and angled patio windows, opposing patios. Carport on left is configured differently from that on the architectural plan (next page). (c) JWS 1958

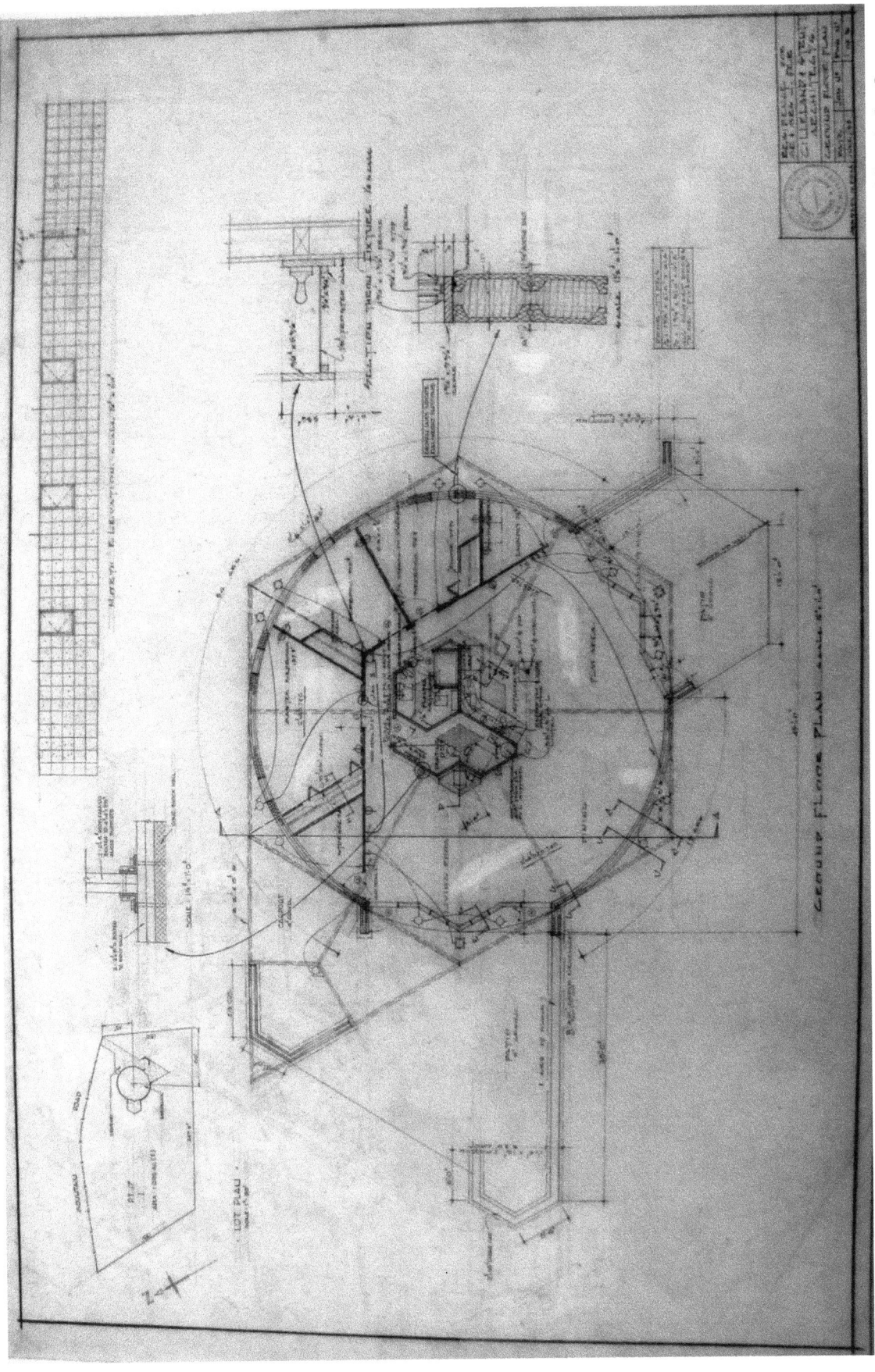

FE house. Triangular parking carport (left), no wing rooms. Note elevation of curved rear wall with four bedroom windows. Note two sets of <u>angled</u> patio windows at opposing sides of the living area. Entry via patio. Note short (one x 16" high) privacy wall at left. (c) JWS 1958

P house rear view showing bedroom windows, with parking carport, no wing rooms. (c) JWS 1959

P house front view with walk-through. Parking carport, no wing rooms. Note visible interior showing fireplace. (c) JWS 1959

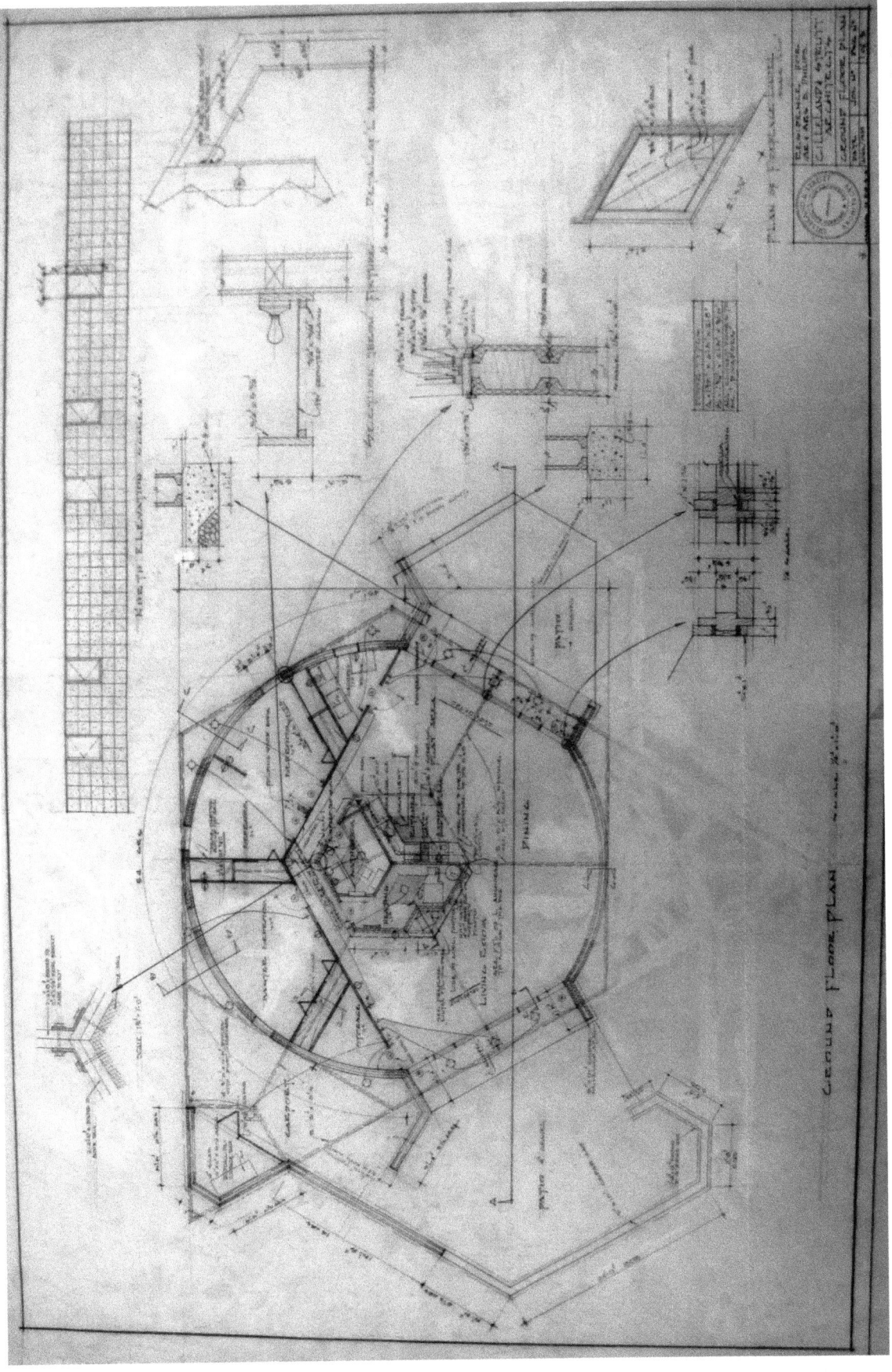

P house. Parking carport, no wing rooms, opposing patio windows. Note elevation of curved rear wall with windows for bedrooms plus one laundry room (right). Entry via left patio; short privacy wall. (c) JWS 1959

V house with drive-through carport, no wing rooms. The carport opening (bottom right) does not seem wide in this drawing but as built it is drive-through. (c) JWS

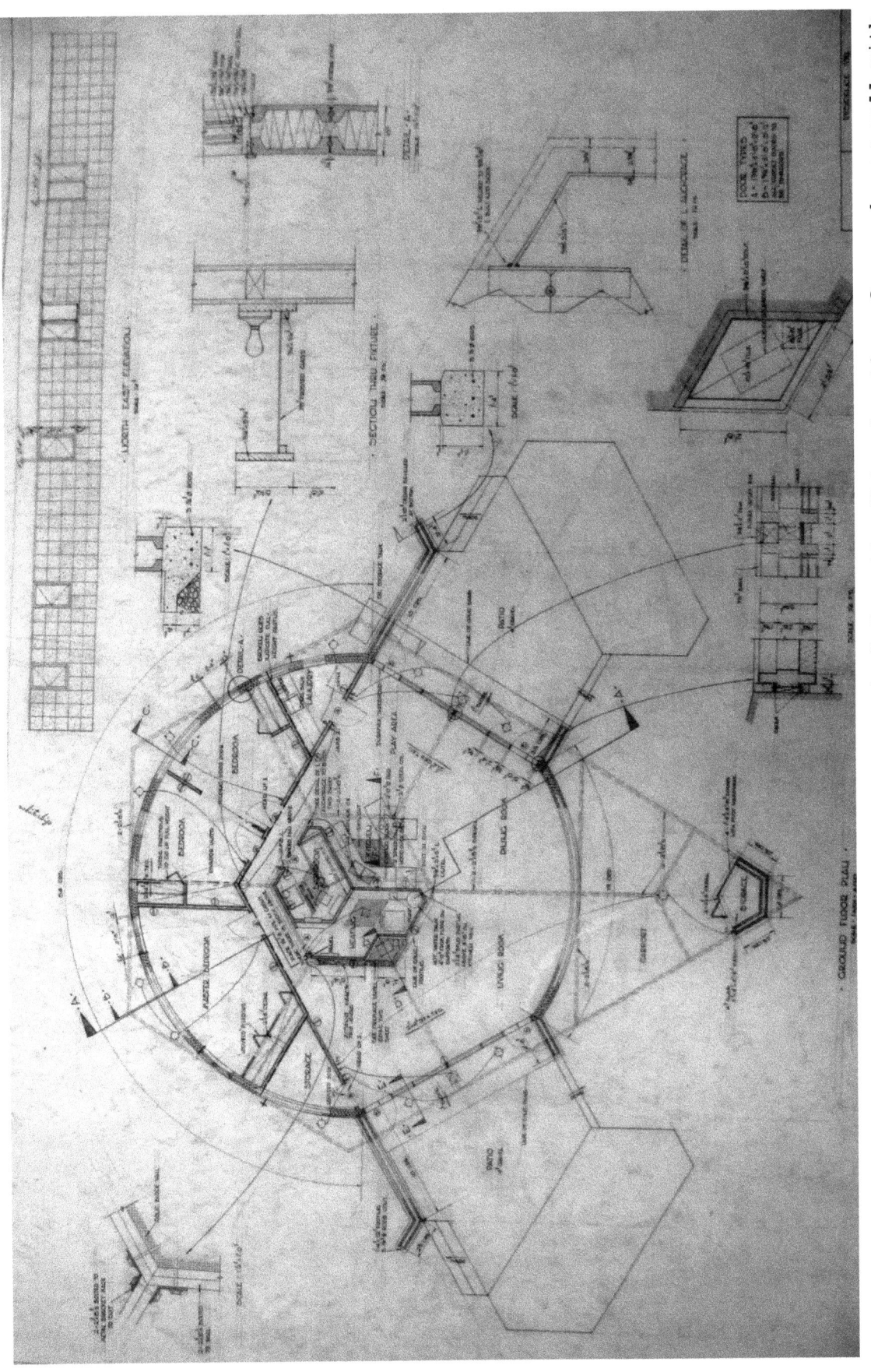

V house. Drive-through carport no wing rooms. Entry via left patio. Note elevation of curved rear wall with windows for two bedrooms (single), two doubles for the master bedroom, plus one laundry room. Note the ends of the privacy walls angle away from the patios. (c) JWS 1959

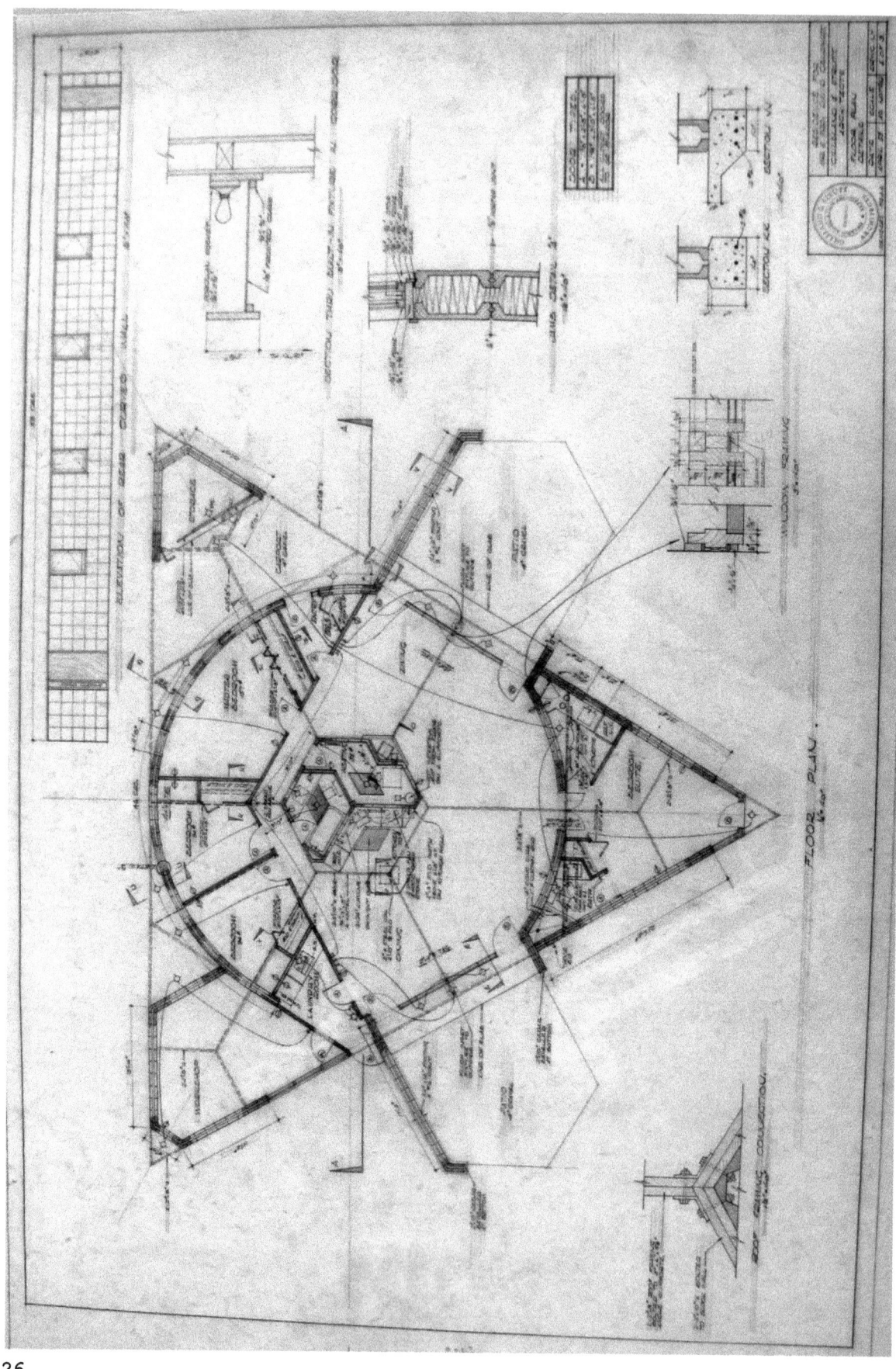

G house. Carport with two wing rooms. Note Block walls as shown were not as built: construction of exterior walls and extending privacy walls were two courses of 4"x8"x16" blocks with a space between. The central core with 120° angles was a single course of blocks. Entrance vestibule at right. Note the ends of the privacy walls angle towards the patios, due to driveway upper right. (c) JWS 1959

G house rear view from the north showing bedroom windows on a curving block
wall, and drive-through carport. Note one of two wing rooms on right.
(c) JWS 1959

(c) James W. Strutt, 1959

G house view from the west, two wing rooms. The back door shows on left.
Note privacy wall; four glass block "windows", not realized. Square blocks
are shown but in the actual construction standard rectangular blocks were
used. Note two patio doors aside windows. (c) JWS 1959

Site plans

The next four configurations here are on different lots, near the Mountain Road, Part of Parcel 17, Range VI, Township of Hull, County of Gatineau, Quebec, proposed.

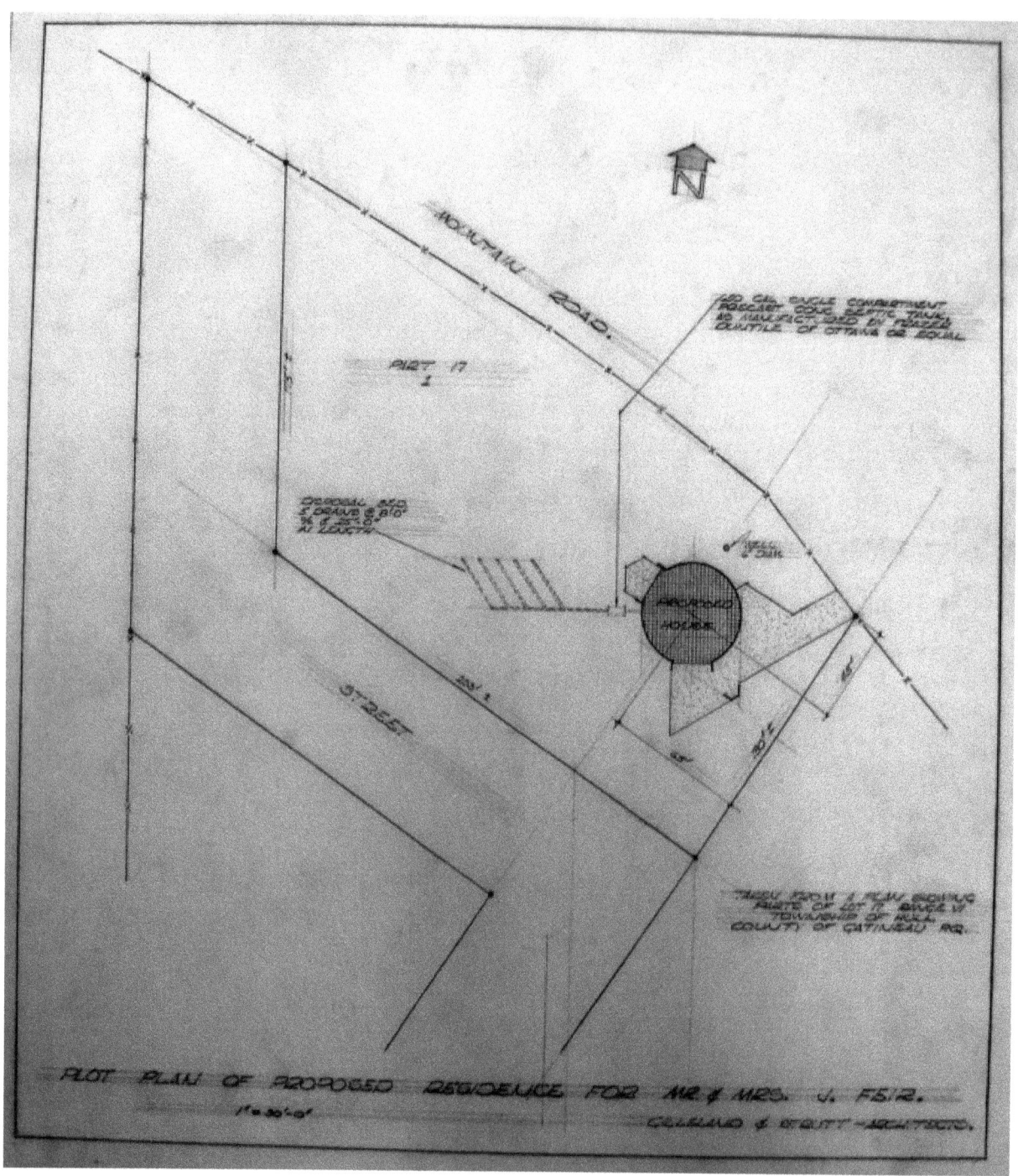

FE house (Part 17 lot 1). No wing rooms, parking carport. (c) JWS 1958

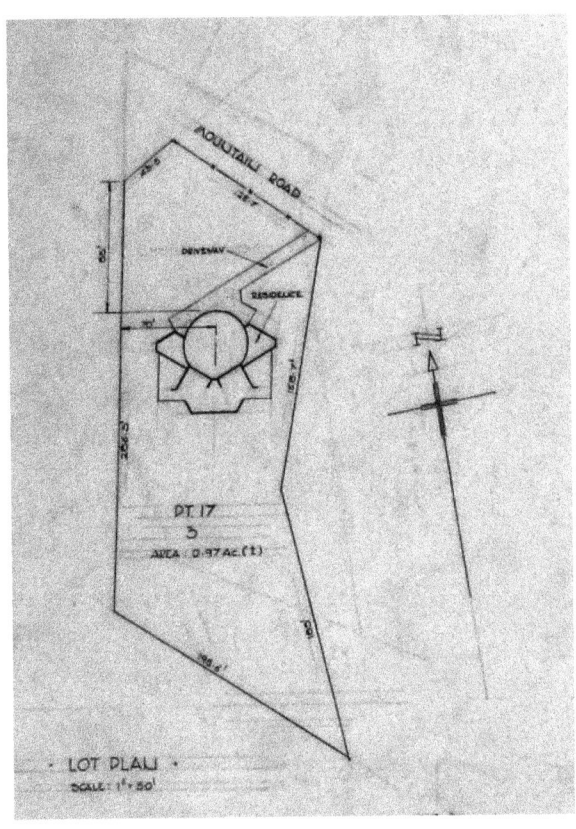

F house (Part 17 lot 3). Two wing rooms, no carport. Note abutting patios and privacy walls. (c) JWS

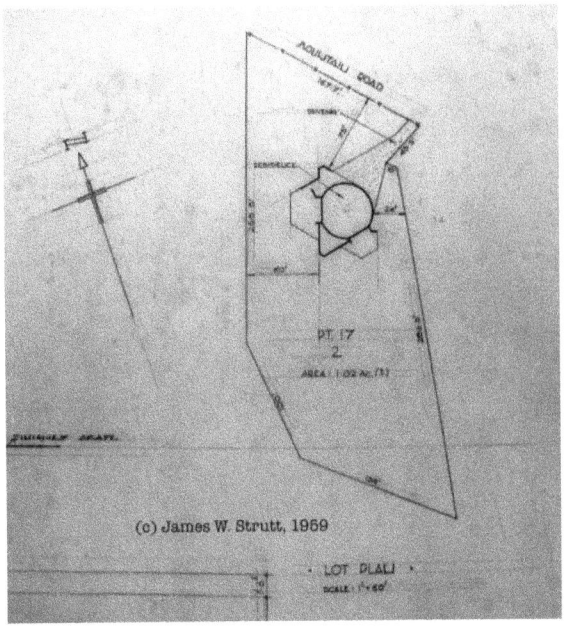

P house variation (Part 17 lot 2) One wing room, with parking carport. (c) JWS 1958

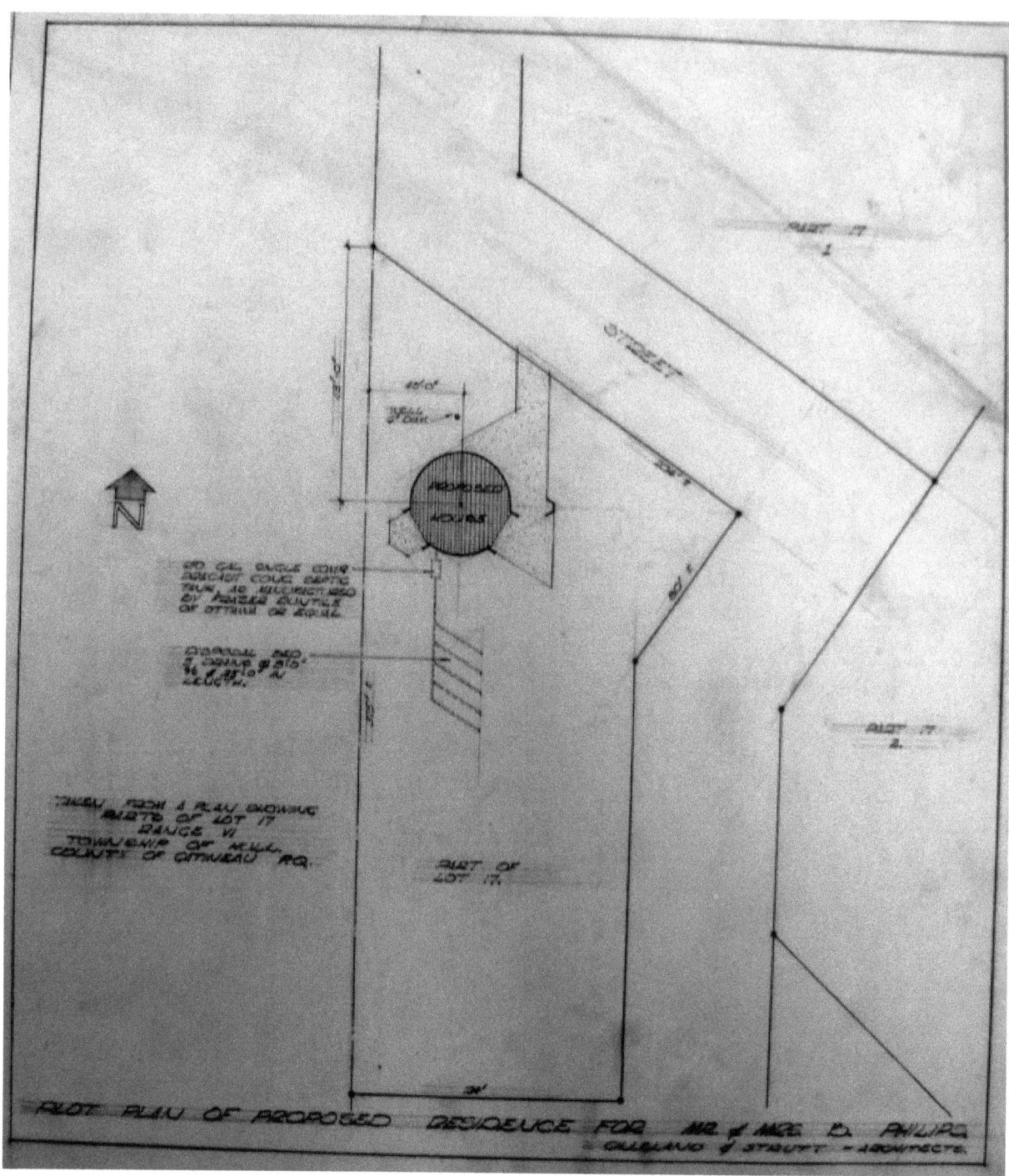

P house (Part 17 lot x). Parking carport, no wing rooms. (c) JWS

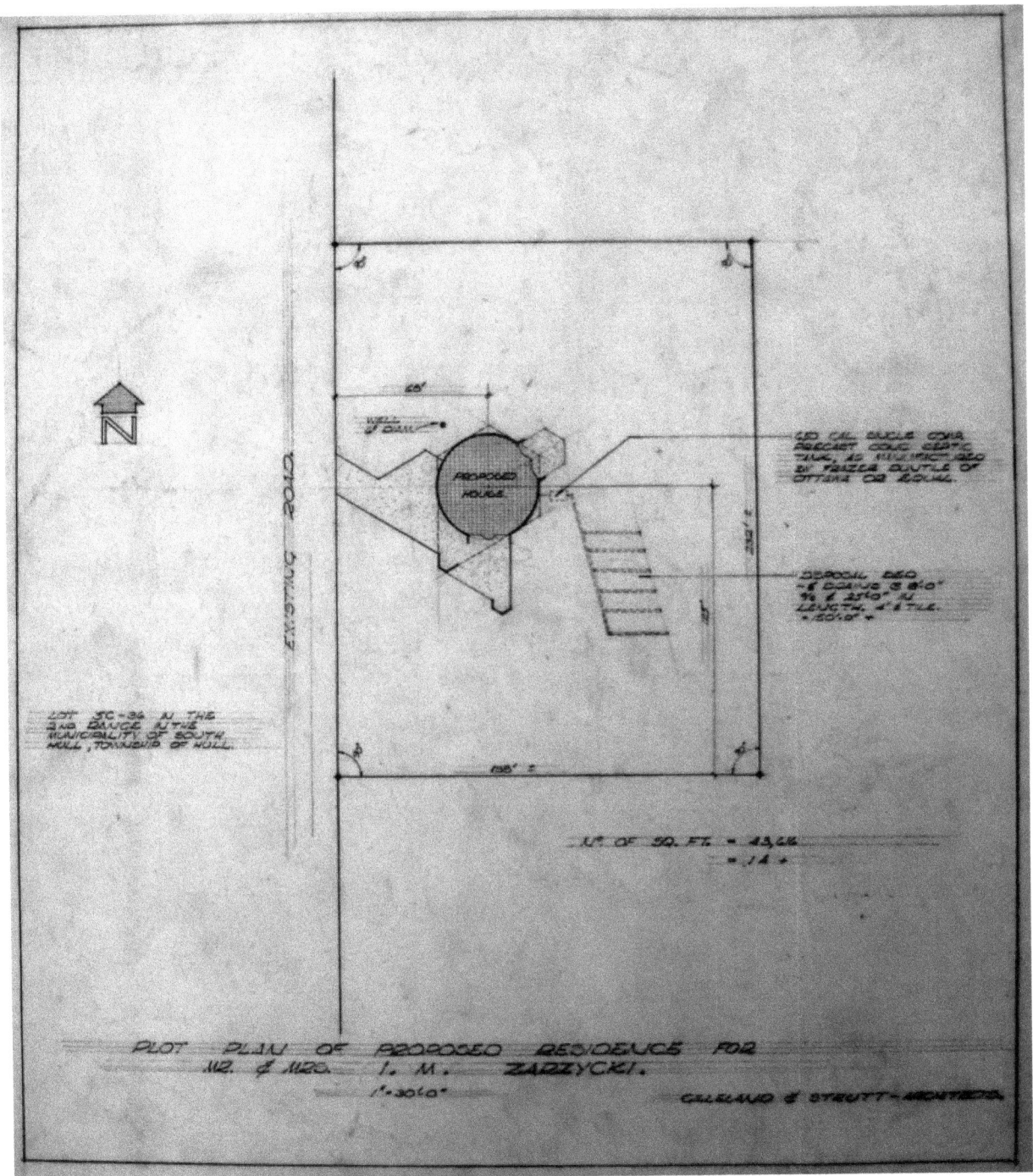

Z house. Parking carport, no wing rooms. (c) JWS

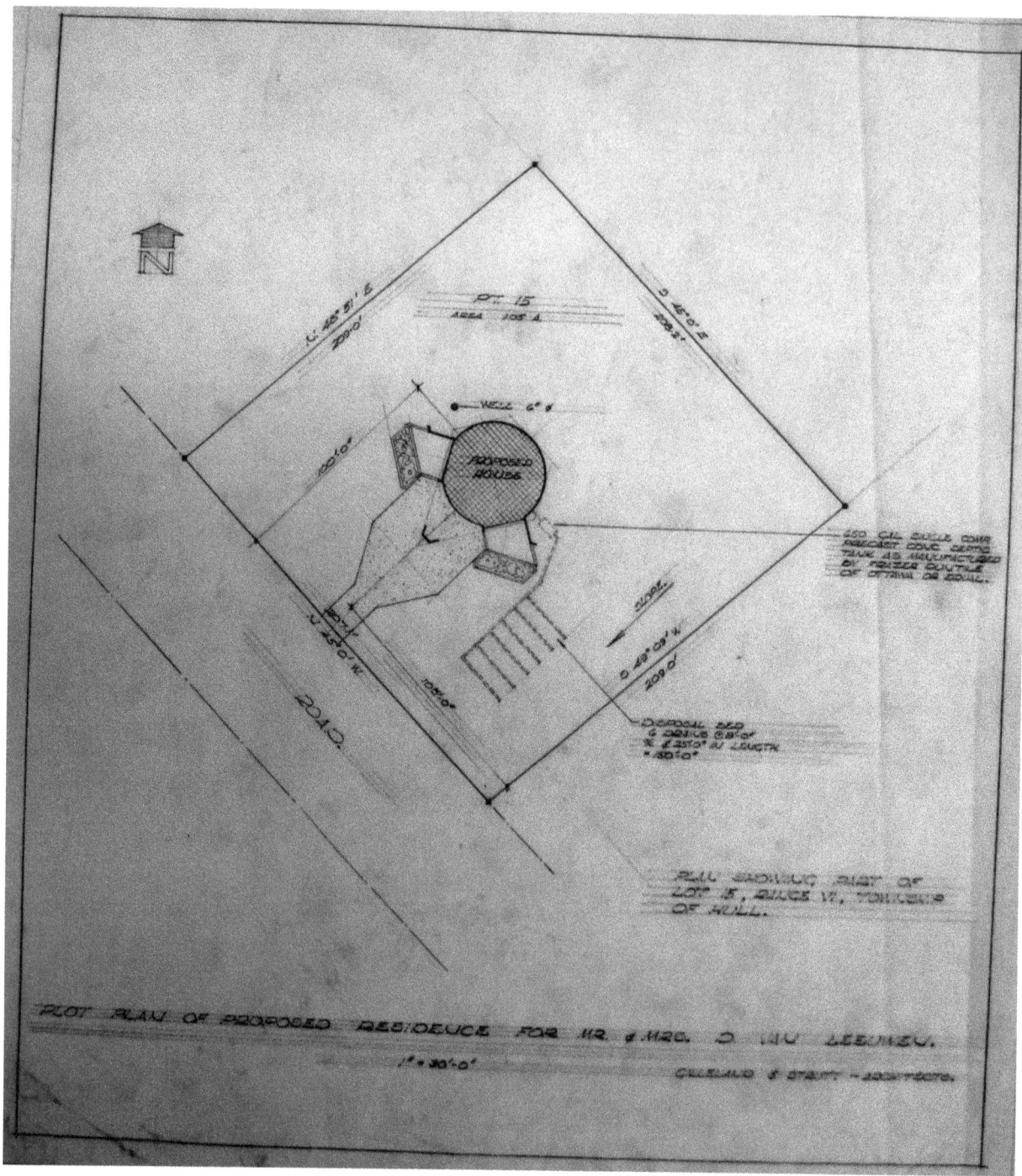

V house. Drive-through carport, no wing rooms. (c) JWS

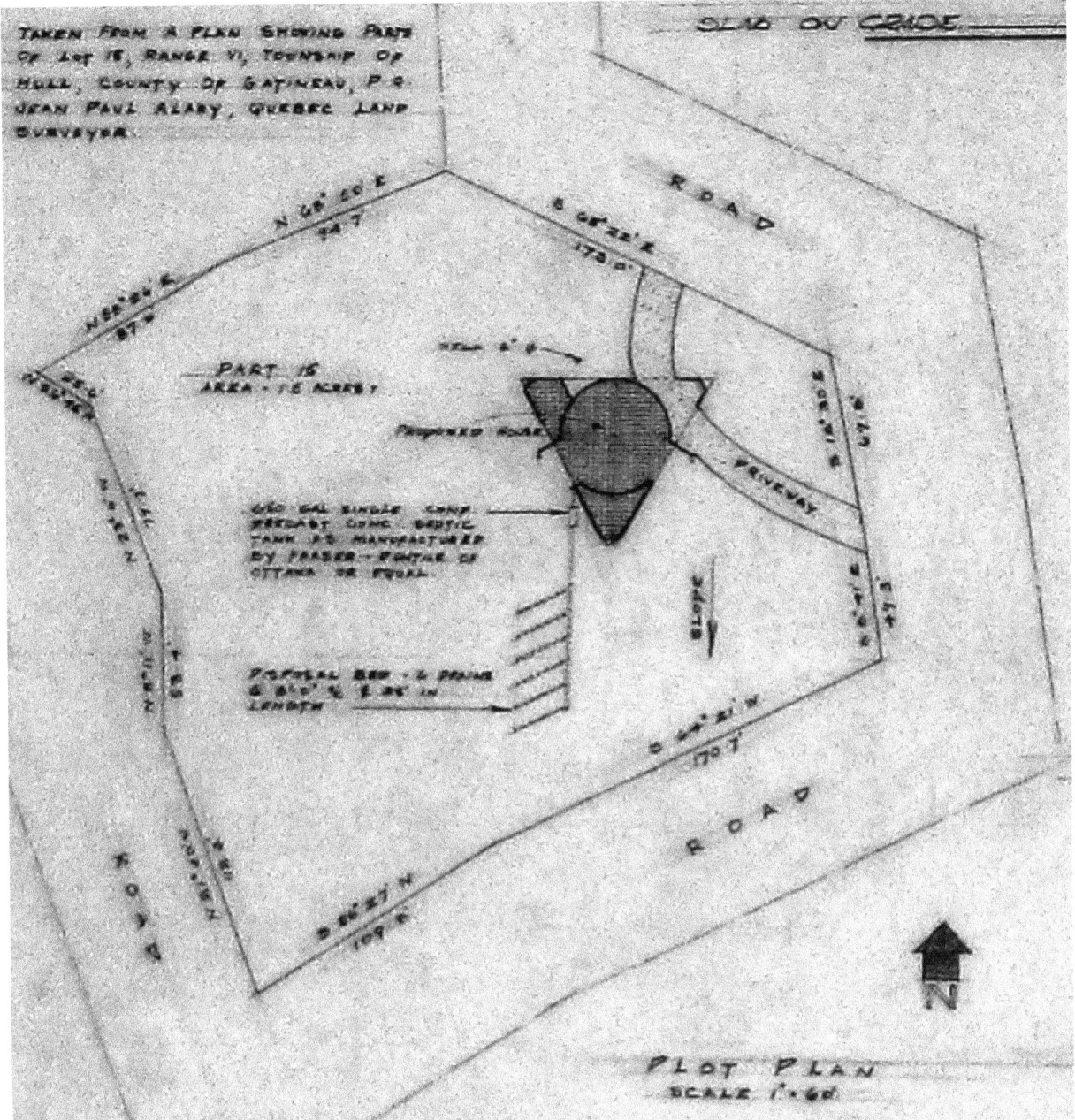

G house plot plan. Drive-through carport and two wing rooms. Note the house points south so that one of the patio windows faces east and the other faces west. (c) JWS

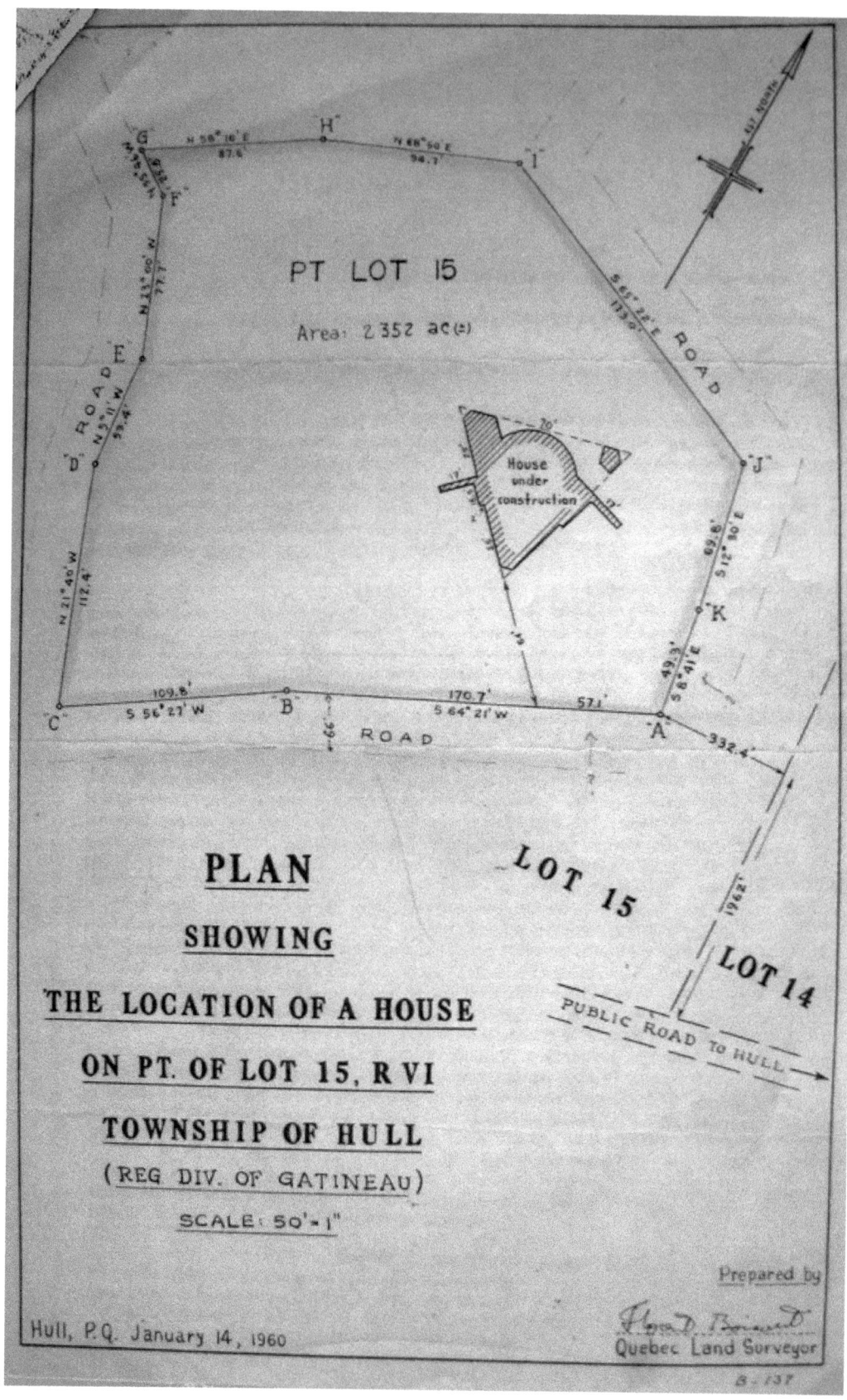

G house Quebec Government Land Survey 1960. Note English only.

G house aerial view c. 2017. Note this shows the covering roof which was added about 1990. (c) Google Earth

Aerial view of the community where two of the round houses (G and V) are located. April 1998.

Elevations

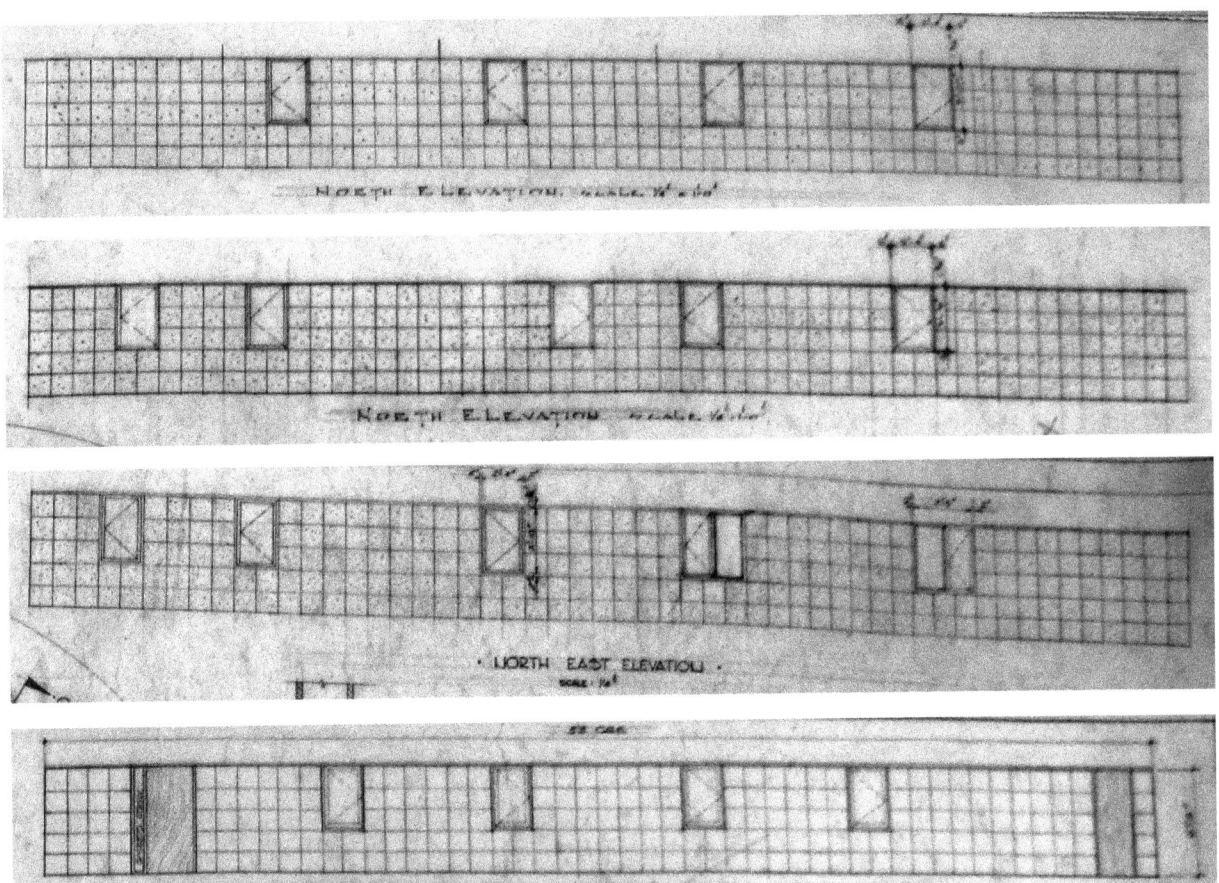

Curved block walls at the rear of the round houses showing bedroom windows and in two cases (middle) a laundry room window. These all show five rows of 16x16 blocks. (c) JWS

Top to bottom: FE house, P house, V house, G house. Note the latter includes front and back doors.

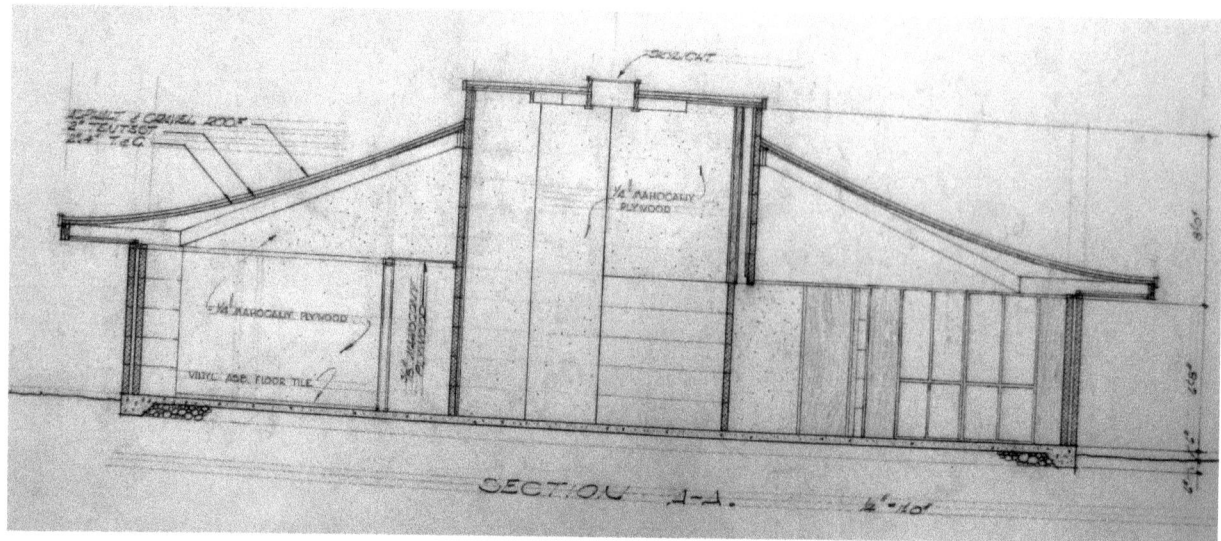

Typical elevation-section. (c) JWS

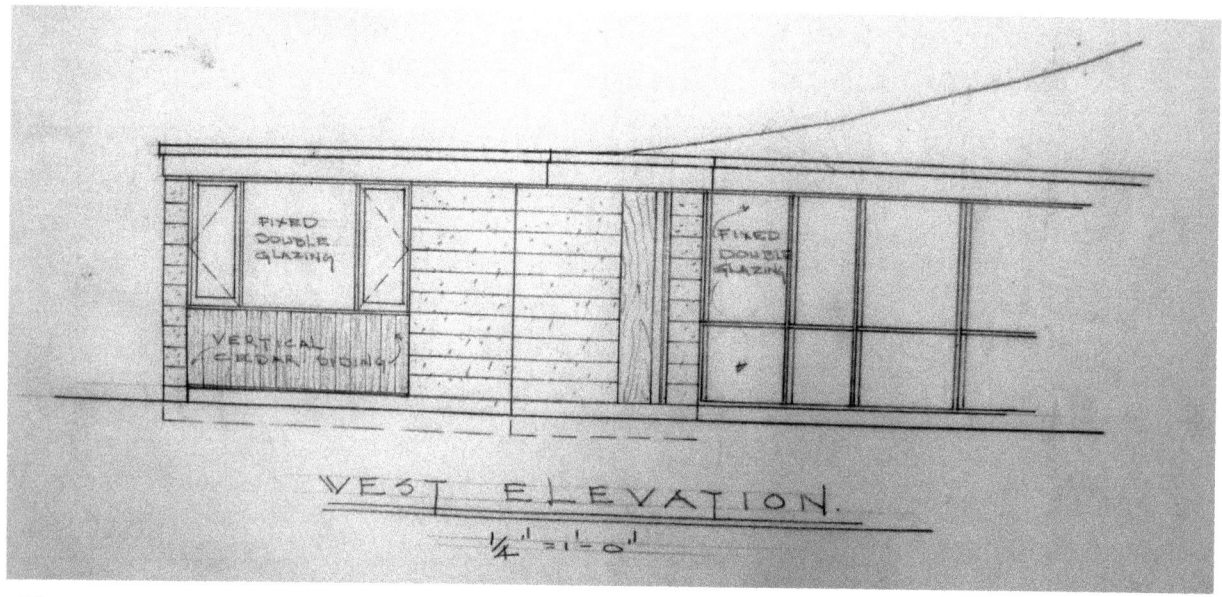

V house elevation. (c) JWS

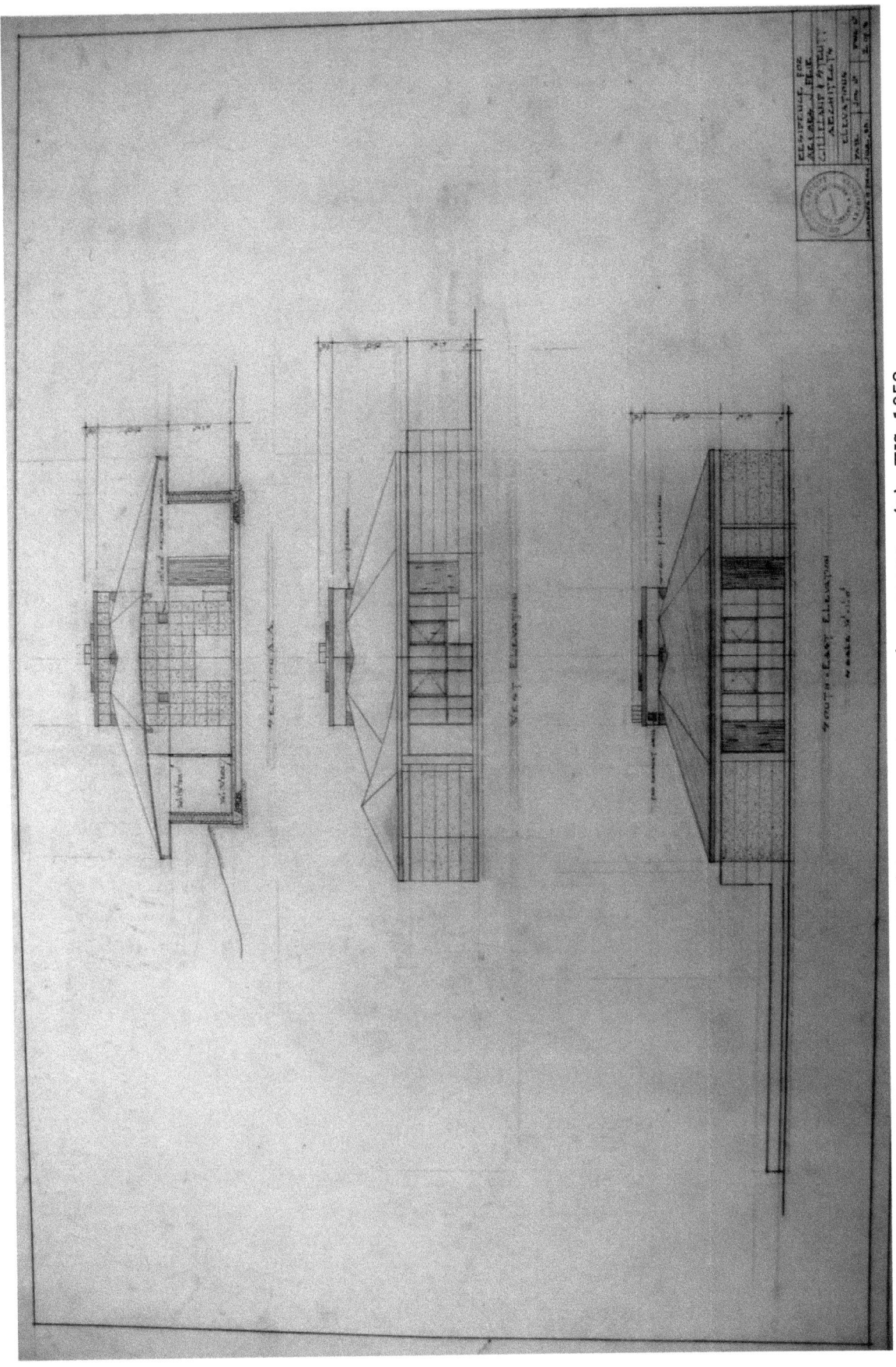

FE house. Section and elevations. Parking carport, no wing rooms. (c) JWS 1958

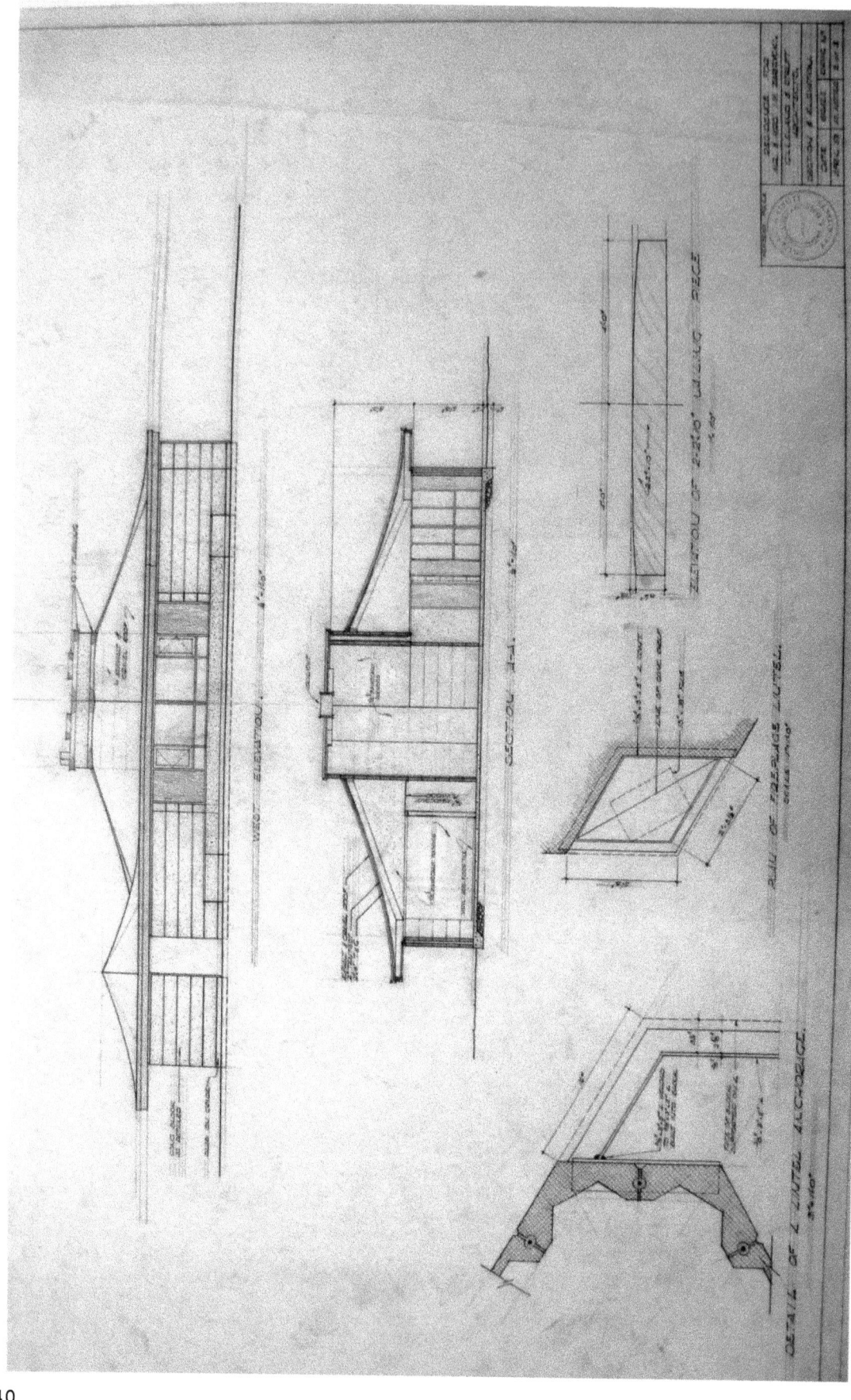

Z house. Elevation, section and details. Parking carport, no wing rooms. Note "Elevation of nailing piece" lower right used to assist in the construction of roofing boards. (c) JWS 1959

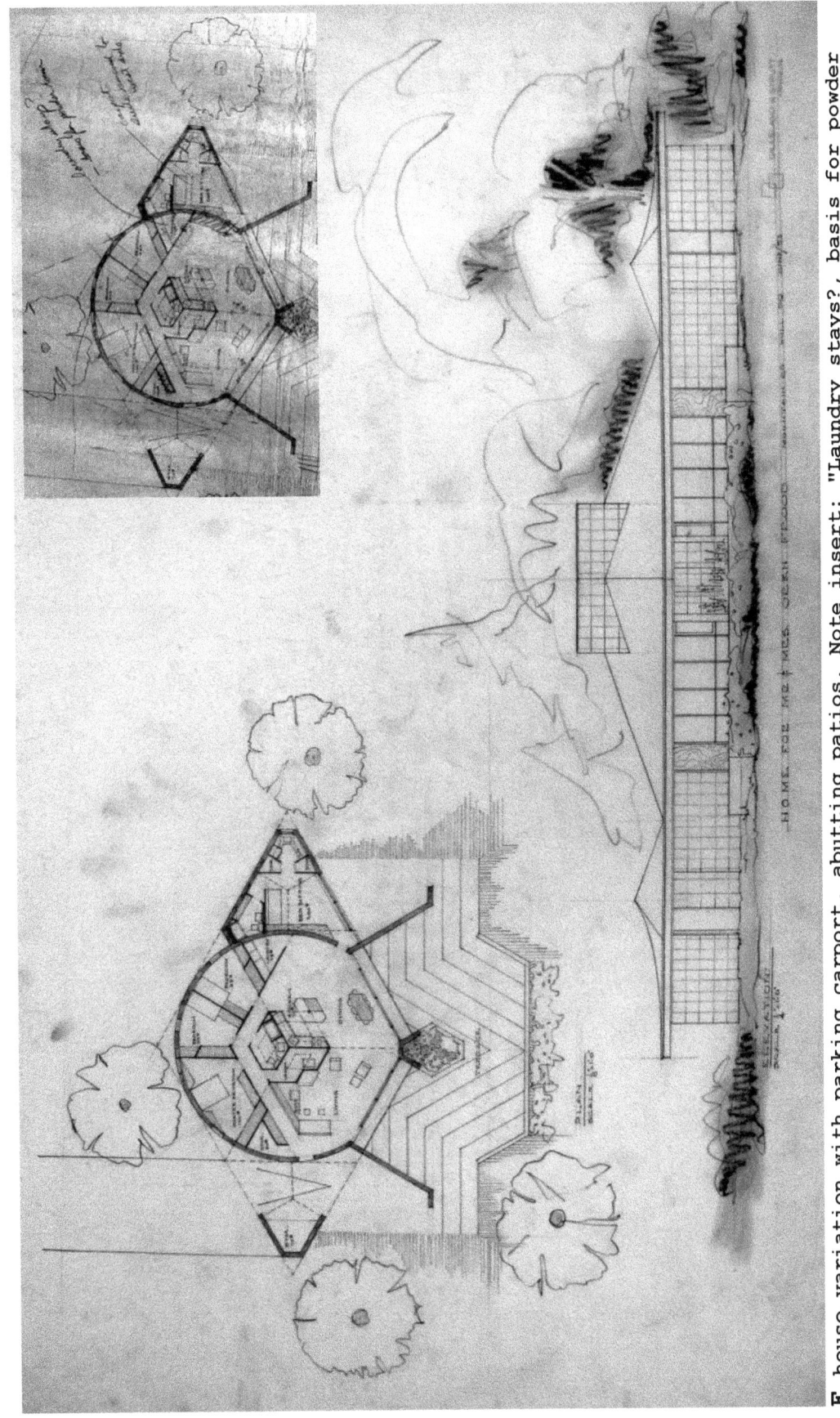

F house variation with parking carport, abutting patios. Note insert: "Laundry stays?, basis for powder room; carport, suite removed to west side." (c) JWS

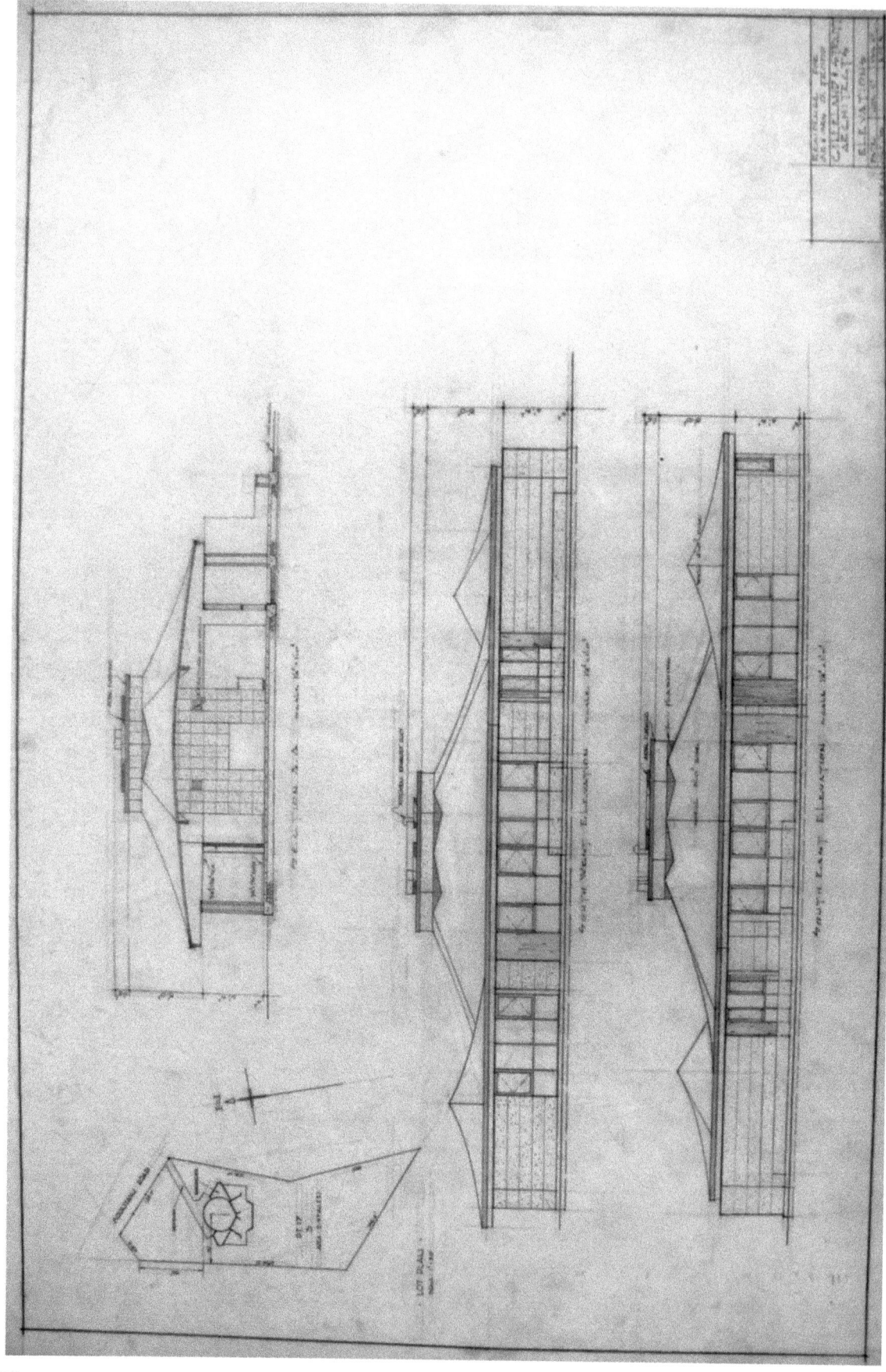

F house. Section and elevations. Two wing rooms, no carport, abutting patios. (c) JWS 1958

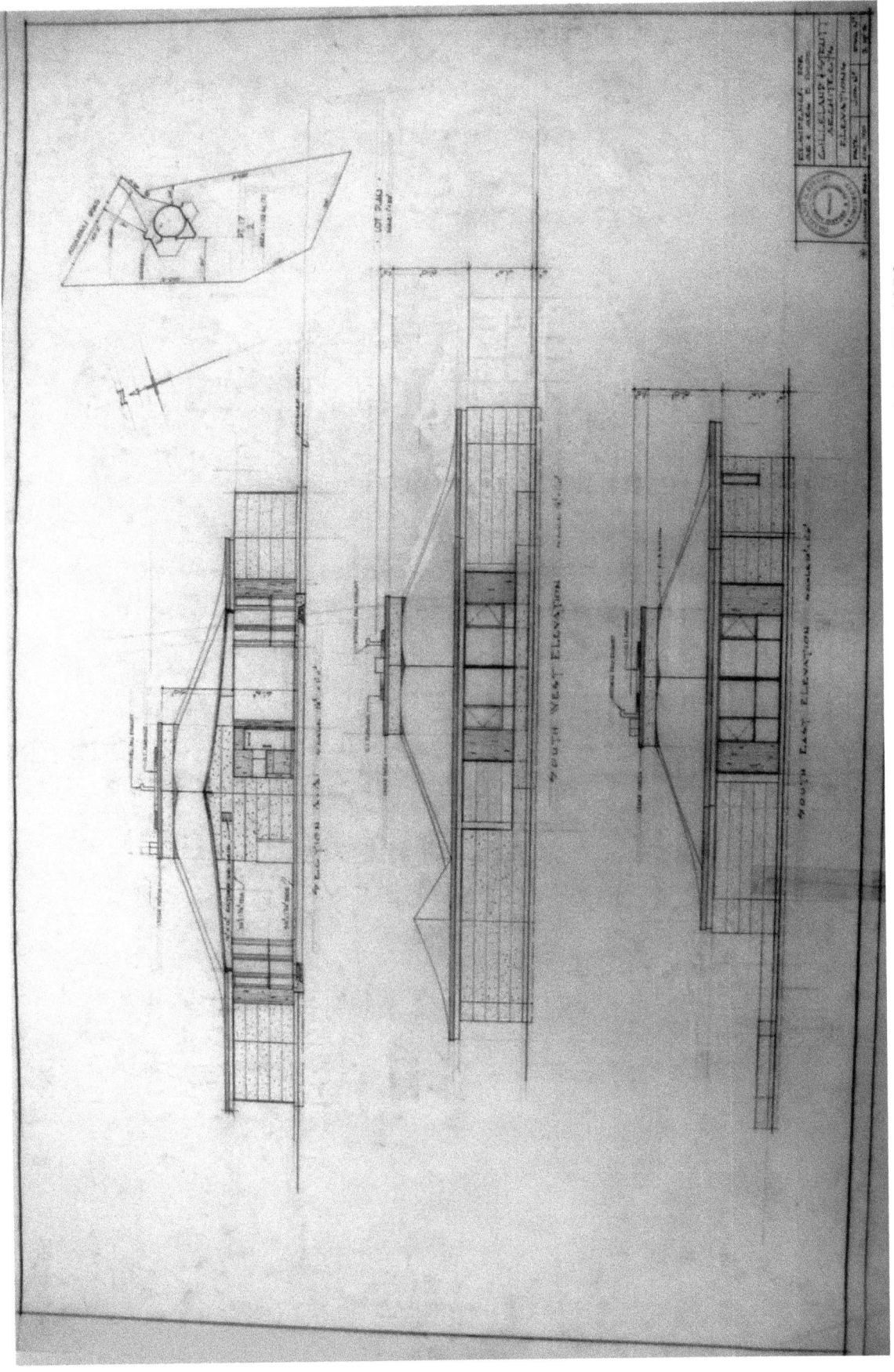

P house variation. Section and elevations. Parking carport, one wing room. (c) JWS 1959

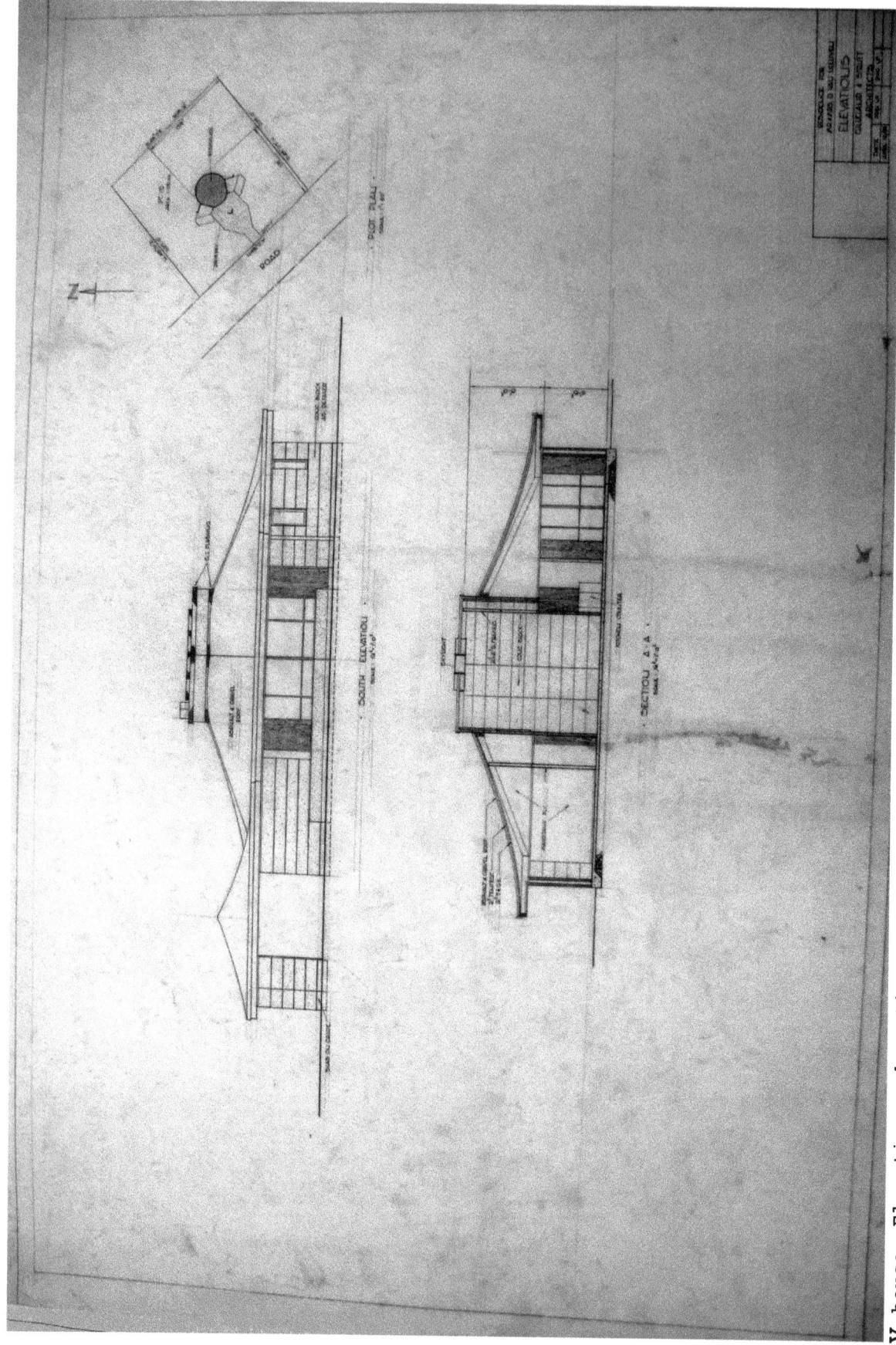

V house. Elevation and section. Drive-through carport, no wing rooms. (c) JWS 1959

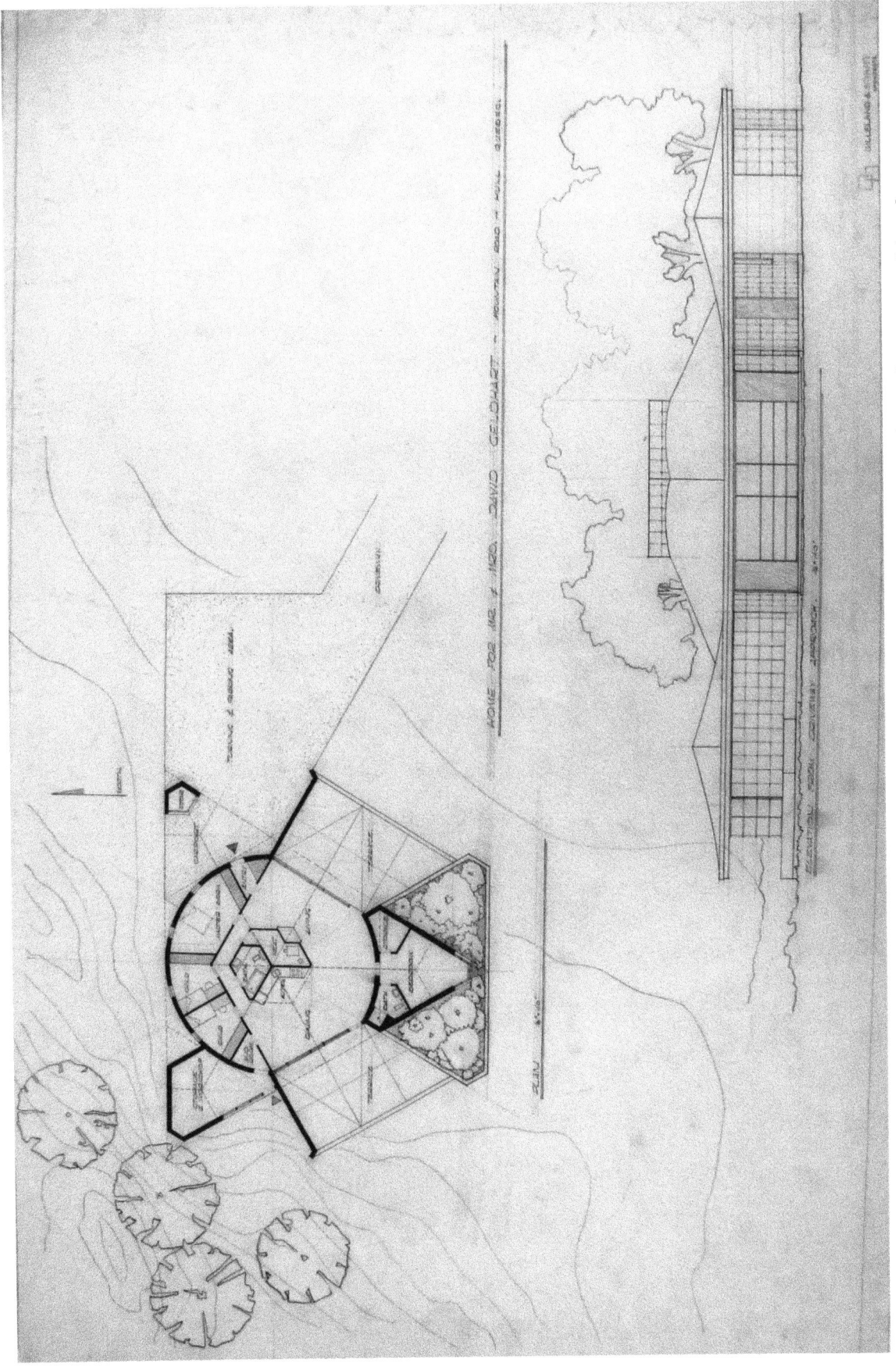

G house presentation plan and elevation. The plan is not as-built: there is only one patio door per terrace; the apartment wing room bathroom is a bit larger than built and "storage" became the kitchenette. The exterior walls came in a bit and there was a short buttress wall (see previous construction drawing). (c) JWS 1959

45

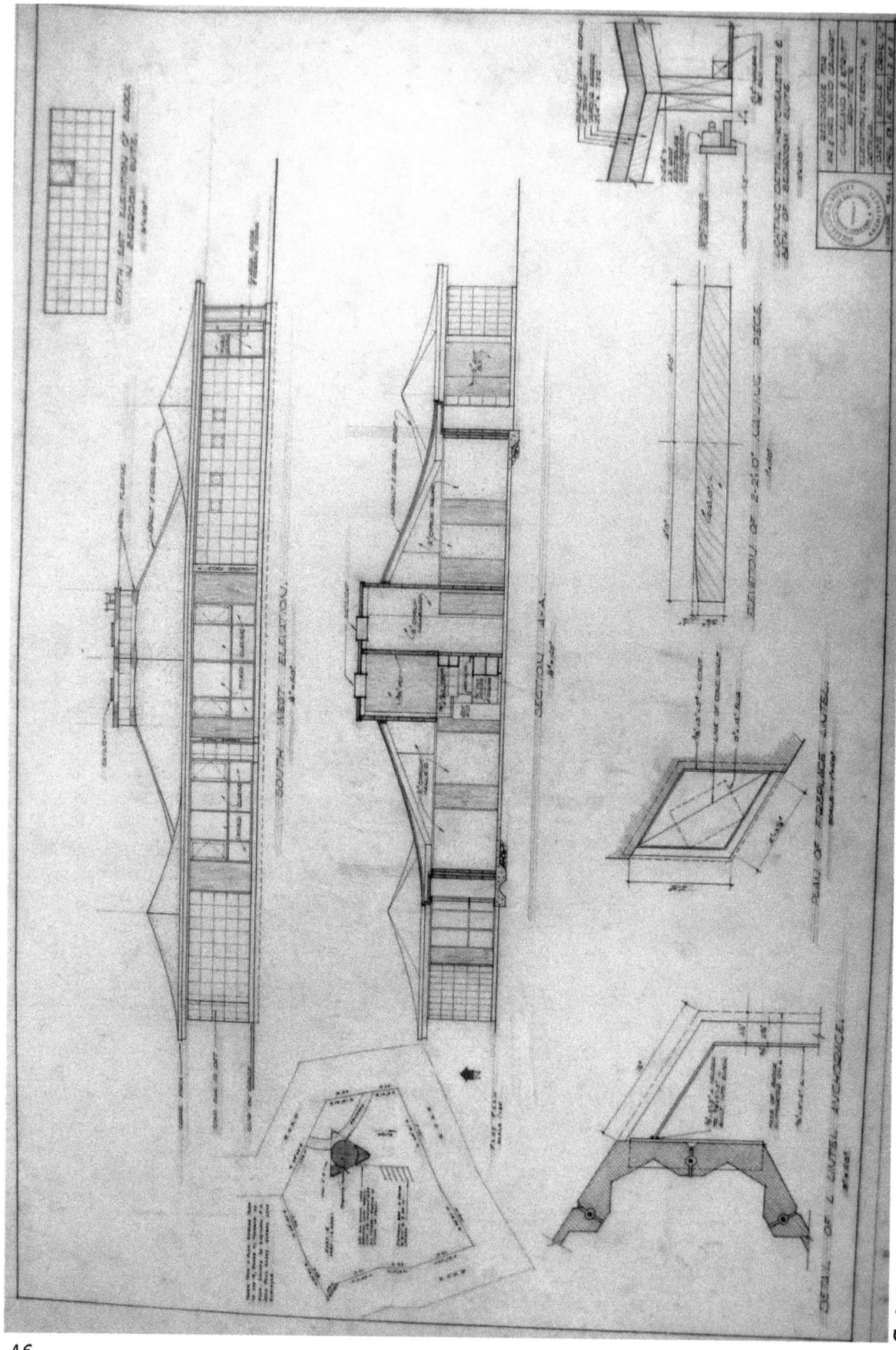

G house. Drive-through carport, two wing rooms. The arrangement shown (top) of two sets of patio doors and windows which abut side-by-side is not as shown on the G plans nor as-built, which is opposing terraces; nor were the four glass block "windows" and the opening window (top). (c) JWS 1959

G house elevations c. 1970-1980.

Sections

Section details can also be found in the other chapters.

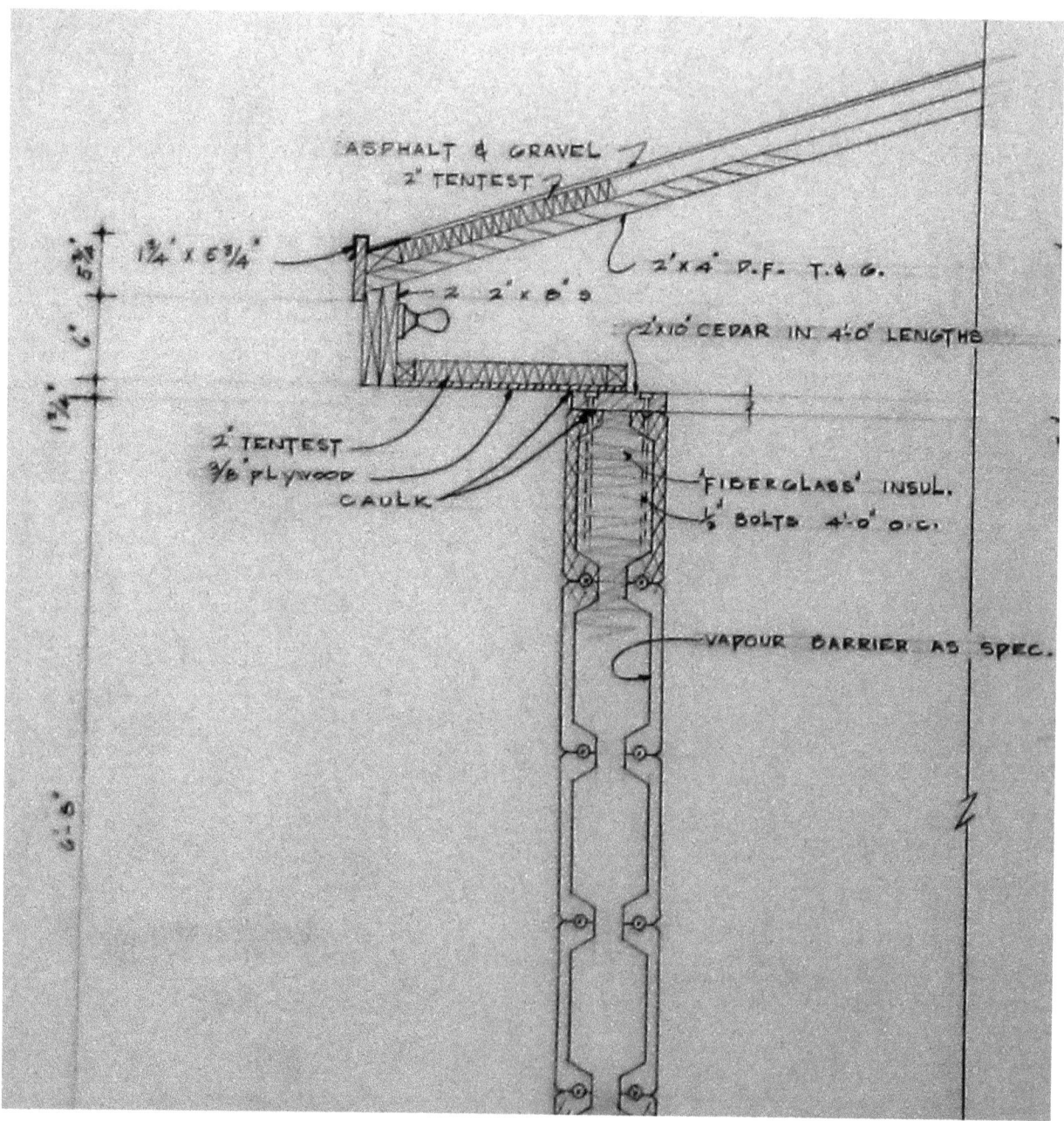

P house wall sections detail showing recessed light. Other houses similar. (c) JWS

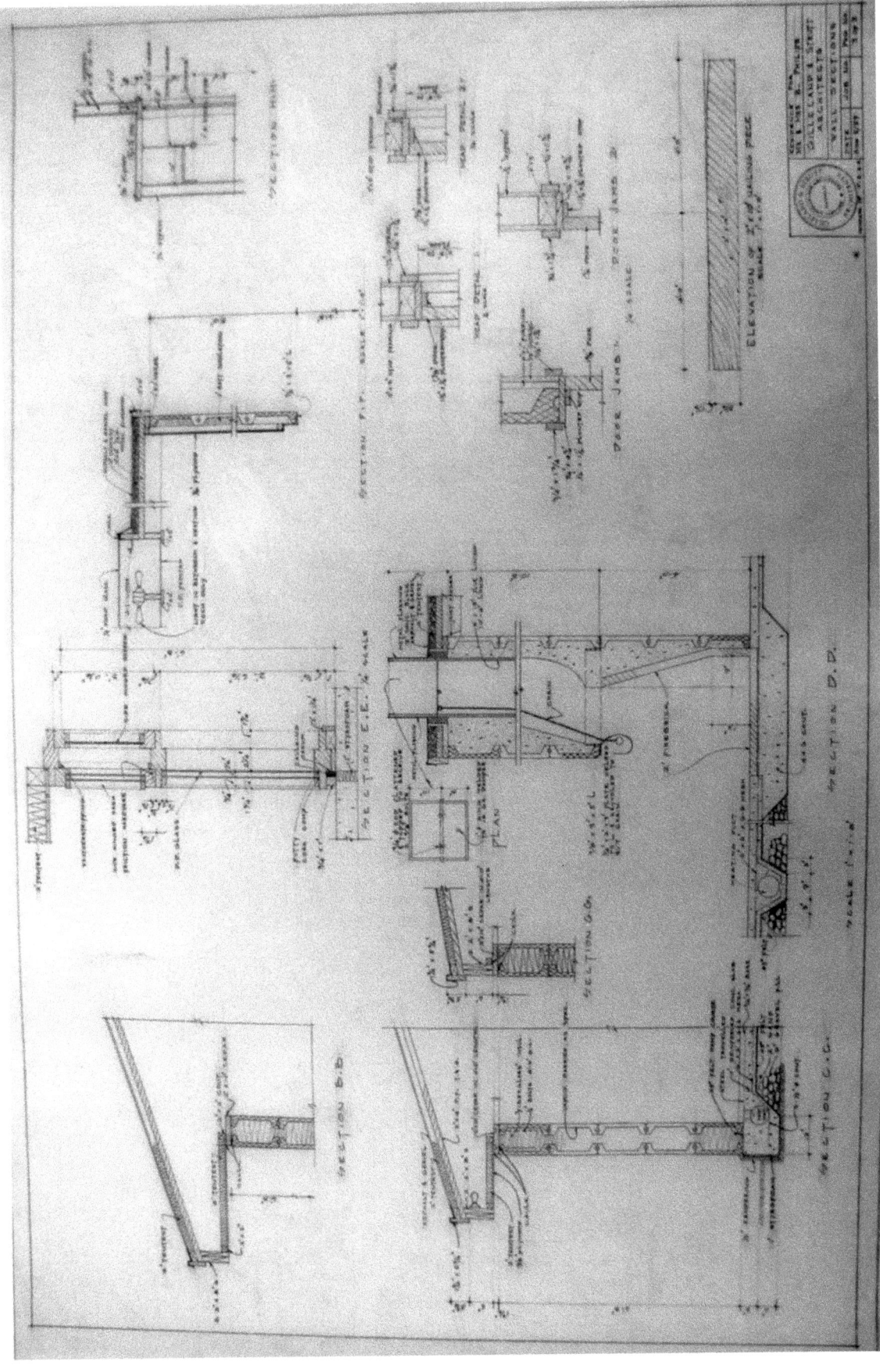

P house sections and details. Other round houses similar. (c) JWS 1959

Foundation

For the G house a concrete slab was poured on a level sand base following the circular outline of the main house (measuring about 45' in diameter), and under the triangular wing rooms. The carport was dirt and gravel and only had concrete under the storage room at the point of its triangle. This whole arrangement was a "floating slab".

The ground was prepared and depressions made where the furnace supply air ducts were laid out emanating from the central core at the furnace exit. The concrete slab was to be heated at the perimeter by virtue of the embedded air supply ducts, as well as along the edges of the base of the two wing rooms.

Inherent problems with this arrangement was that the concrete tended to degrade at the underside resulting in the ingress of sand and dirt which could block the passage of the air around the circuit.

Water supply from the wellhead ran to the central furnace room and thence to the kitchen, bathroom, laundry and apartment suite. It had to run at a depth of a couple of feet rising to just under carport and the front door in order to enter the furnace room floor. This was not deep enough and was liable to freeze in winter since a snow cover was not left in this area. Plumbing copper pipes and lead drains were laid out to run within the poured concrete slab with a main drain to the septic tank making remedial work impossible. Improved insulation would be needed. See the Rebuild chapter.

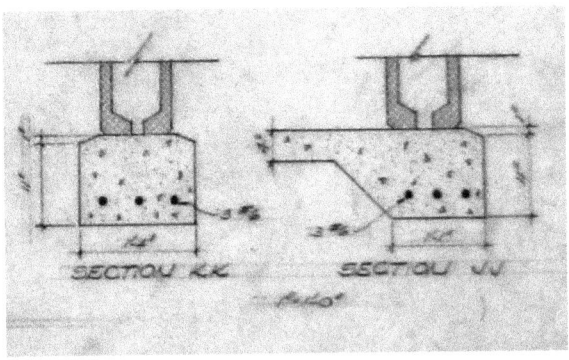

G house section at footing. (c) JWS

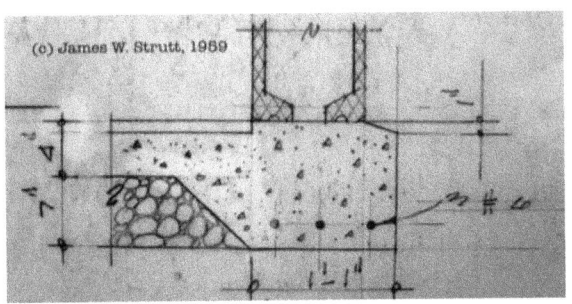

P & V houses Footing Section. Note:
no heating duct in this portion of
the house perimeter. (c) JWS

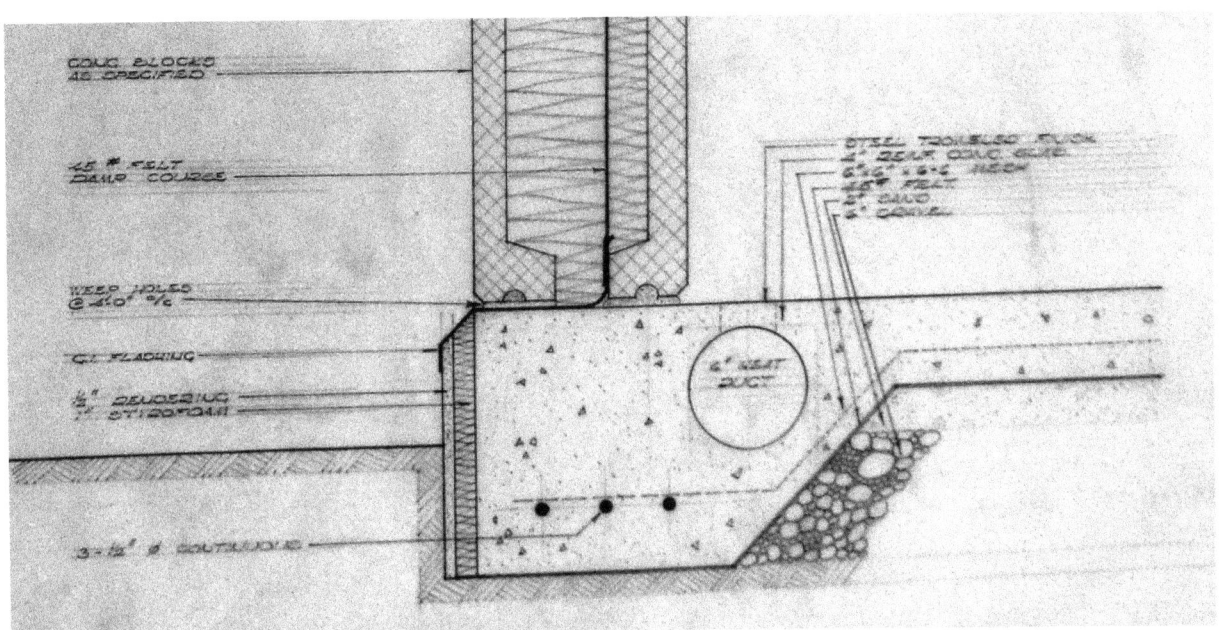

Round houses typical wall section at base around perimeter, detail. Note 6"
forced air heating air supply duct. (c) JWS 1959

Efficiency of the hot air supply system

   This diagram shows that the owner examined the efficiency of the heating ducts in the concrete floor slab. It shows there was a reduction in air flow due to partial collapse of the ducts around the perimeter.

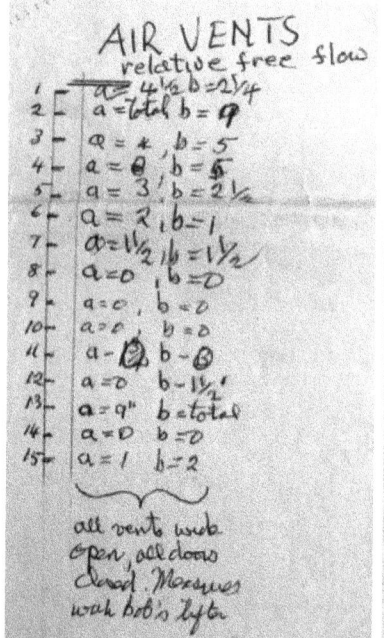

G house. Measurement of air flow through floor heating supply ducts, by owner. c. 1980

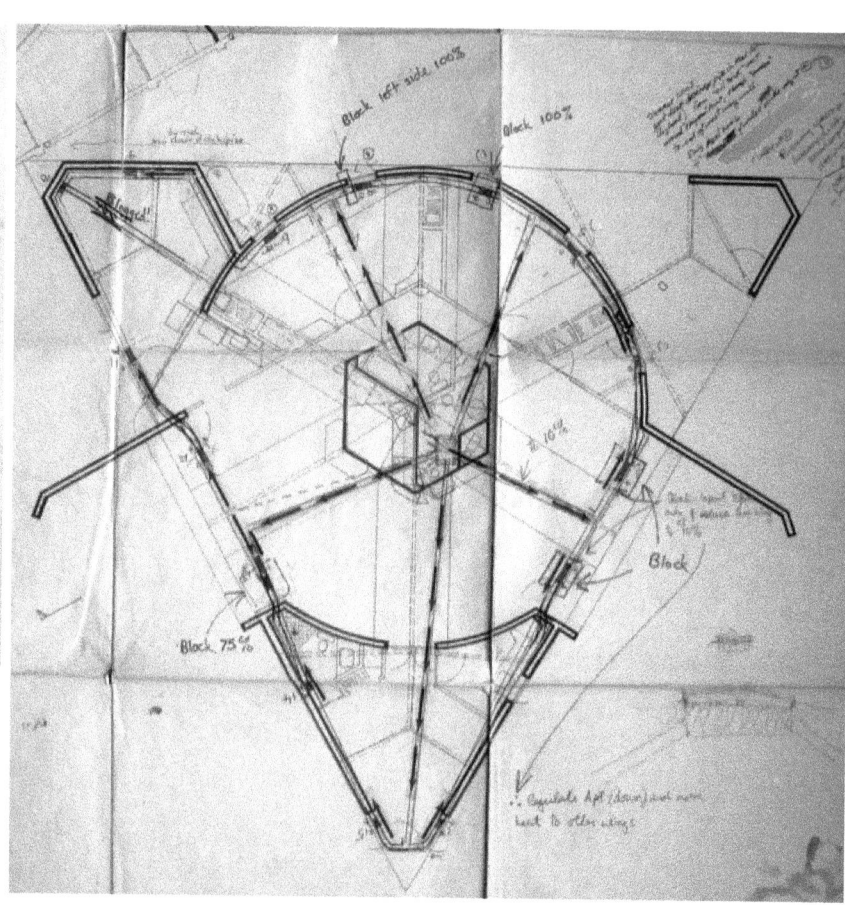

G house. Diagram of heating supply ducts embedded in the concrete floor, by owner. c. 1980

Initial layout of the circular form and a wing room in background. 1959

Preparation of routing for air supply ducts. Note wire mesh. 1959

Central core furnace hot air supply exit; well water supply. Note wire mesh. 1959

Supply heating ducts placed around perimeter of slab form. Note rebar. 1959

G house

Preparing ground for ducts in floating slab. 1959

Block walls

The round house architectural drawings show walls of two courses of 4"x16"x16" precast cement blocks, creating an inner cavity. These would have had a smooth outside finish. There was a vapour barrier "as specified" on the inside surface of the inner blocks. The blocks were drafted on the elevations as a symmetrical grid of 16x16 blocks evenly stacked one on the other, not staggered. He specified "Cross ties - No. 10 galvanized wire @16" o/c". Further, in some houses "pierced block" windows indicate that blocks were replaced by glass blocks in the form of a pattern.

However, the photos of the G house show exterior walls of ten rows of two courses of 4"x8"x16" blocks with a 2" space between. These naturally had a rough finish. These were a modification introduced just before materials were ordered and construction begun because the larger square blocks are on the G house plans. Either the manufacturer could not deliver at the time or it was determined with the builder that the larger blocks would have been unstable or difficult to secure, or it was a matter of cost (a single course of 8"x16" blocks would suffice for un-insulated inner walls such as the hexagon tower). On the G & V houses as-built the 8x16 blocks were staggered.

Contrary to the plans, the following *Typical Wall Section* dated November 1959 shows 4"x8"x16" blocks. Compare this with the blocks shown on the facing page and the section drawing in the Roof chapter dated August 1959 which show 4"x16"x16" blocks.

In the G house as built, rock wool insulation was placed in this intervening space in the exterior walls but it tended to settle over time, leaving the upper half of the walls not sufficiently insulated for Canadian winters.

The central block hexagon of 8'-wide sides is a single course of 4"x8"x16" blocks. The angle where they meet is 120°; corners simply dovetail. The walls are 20 rows up to the HP ceiling and four additional rows up to the slightly pitched "flat" roof.

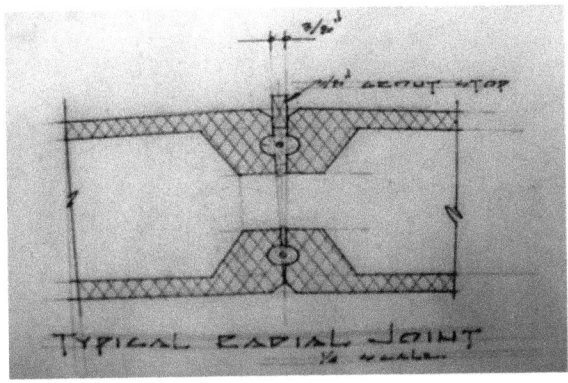

FE house, others similar. Block walls joint spacer to achieve overall wall curvature. (c) JWS 1958

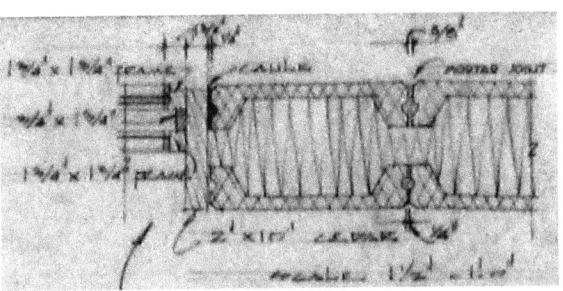

F house, others similar. Block wall to window joint. Note 5/8" mortar joint to achieve overall wall curvature. 1959 (c) JWS

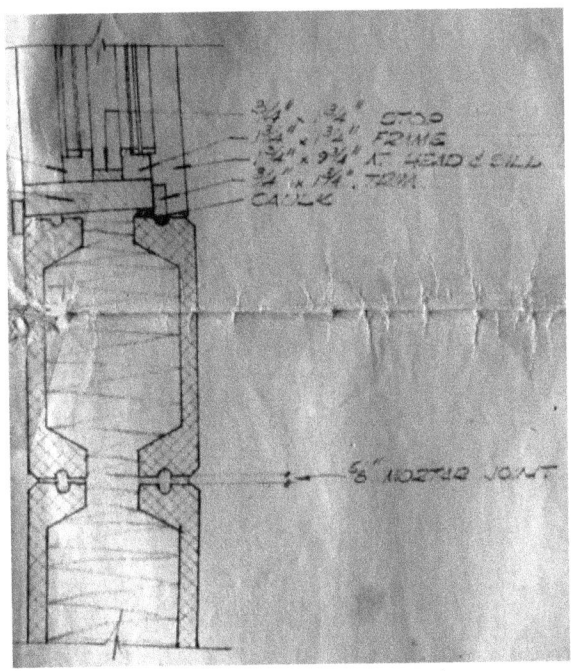

G house Jamb Detail, Note 5/8" mortar joint to achieve overall wall curvature. The blocks used as-built were different (see text). (c) JWS 1959

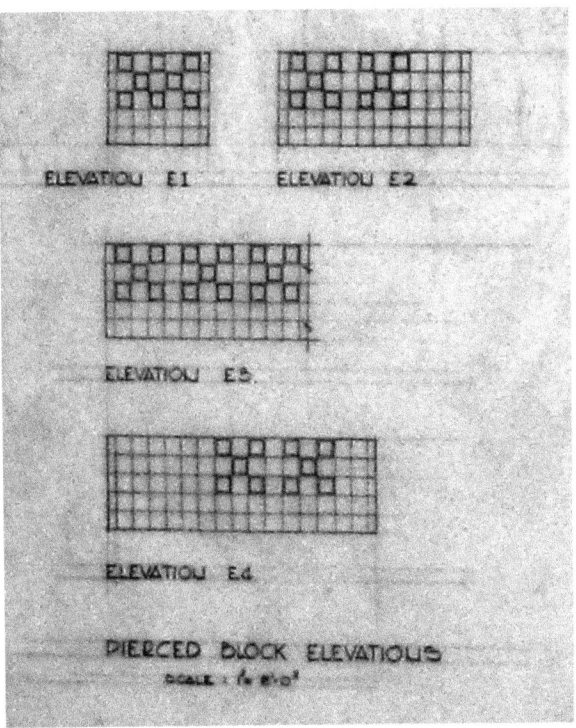

F house showing patterns of block walls where certain concrete blocks were replaced with glass blocks. Detail (c) JWS

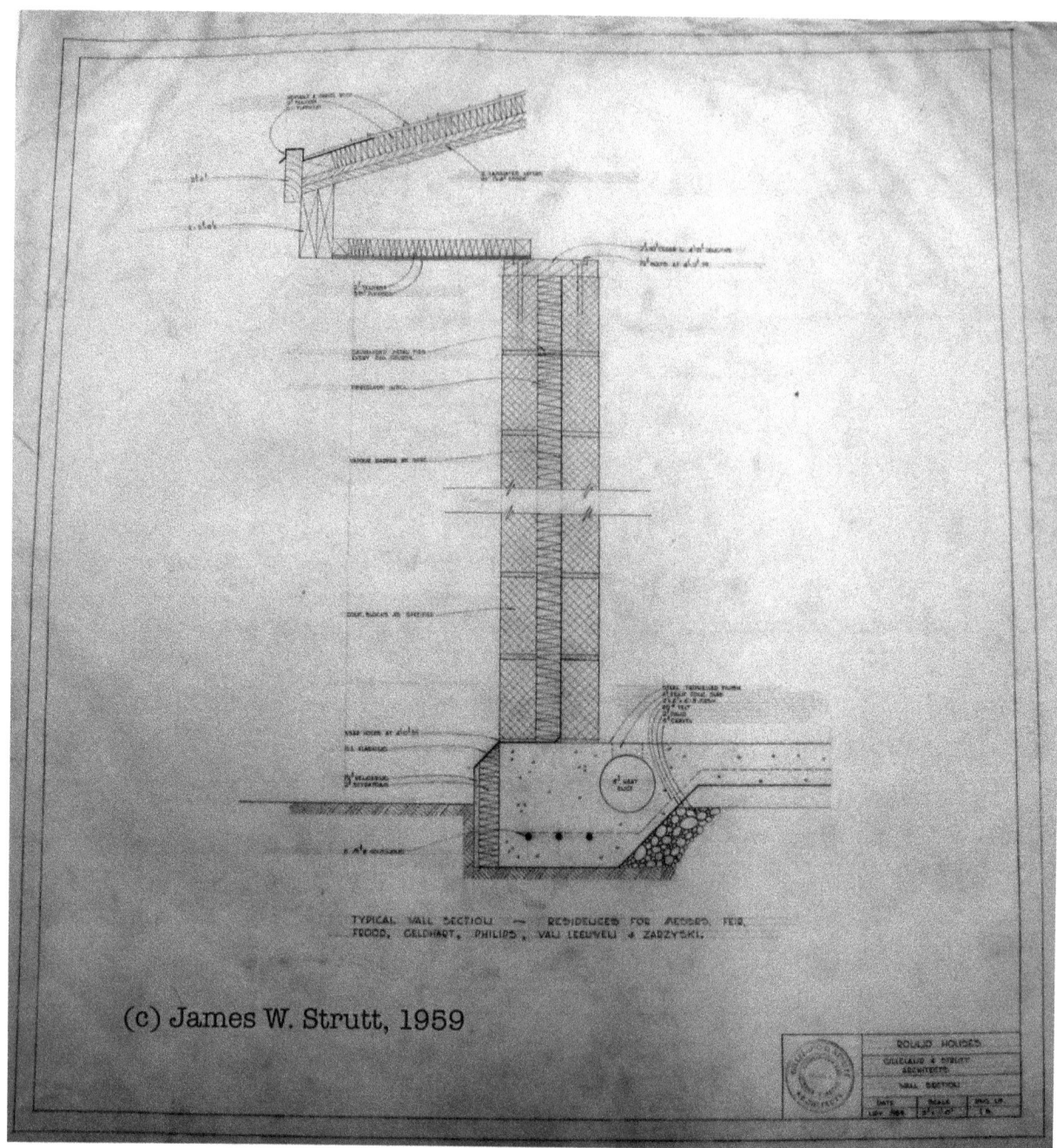

Typical Wall Section showing two courses of 4"x8"x16" blocks with an intervening 2" space for Fiberglass insulation. Compare with the section drawing having 4"x16"x16" blocks in the Roof chapter, page 62. (c) JWS November 1959

Block walls: one wing room in the foreground and a second wing room in the background showing a double-door opening. Full-height central core partially showing the kitchen area. 1959

Central core single-course block walls at kitchen. Note permanent supporting post up from kitchen island. Note dovetailing corners (120°). 1960

Cutting blocks. 1959

Laying one of two courses of the exterior curved wall. 1959

Constructing wing room exterior wall. Note 4"x8"x16" blocks. 1959

G house

Roof

Strutt used a hyperbolic paraboloid (HP) roof membrane of tongue-and-groove (T&G) cedar boards in the round houses. There was no attic or cold air space or insulation other than 2" tentest and tar and gravel. To achieve light weight he used pairs of long boards laminated and nailed together one layer transverse to the other arranged to curve in two directions over one roof section, of which there were six.

The central hexagon extends four block rows above the surrounding sloping roof and has a slightly angled roof with tar and gravel. There is a bathroom vent pipe, fireplace chimney and three diamond-shaped skylights.

For further information on HP structures see:
https://en.wikipedia.org/wiki/Paraboloid and
https://en.wikipedia.org/wiki/Saddle_roof

In the following editorial piece "HP Roofs for Houses" from *Progressive Architecture* 42-8, 1961, Strutt's roofs are discussed. The public source is https://usmodernist.org/.

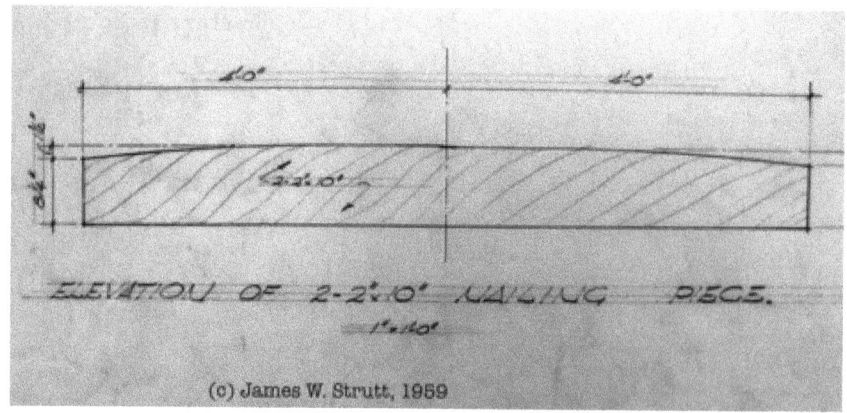

(c) James W. Strutt, 1959

Round houses. Elevation of nailing piece used to guide the laminating and nailing of ceiling boards, thereby giving the required curve. (c) JWS

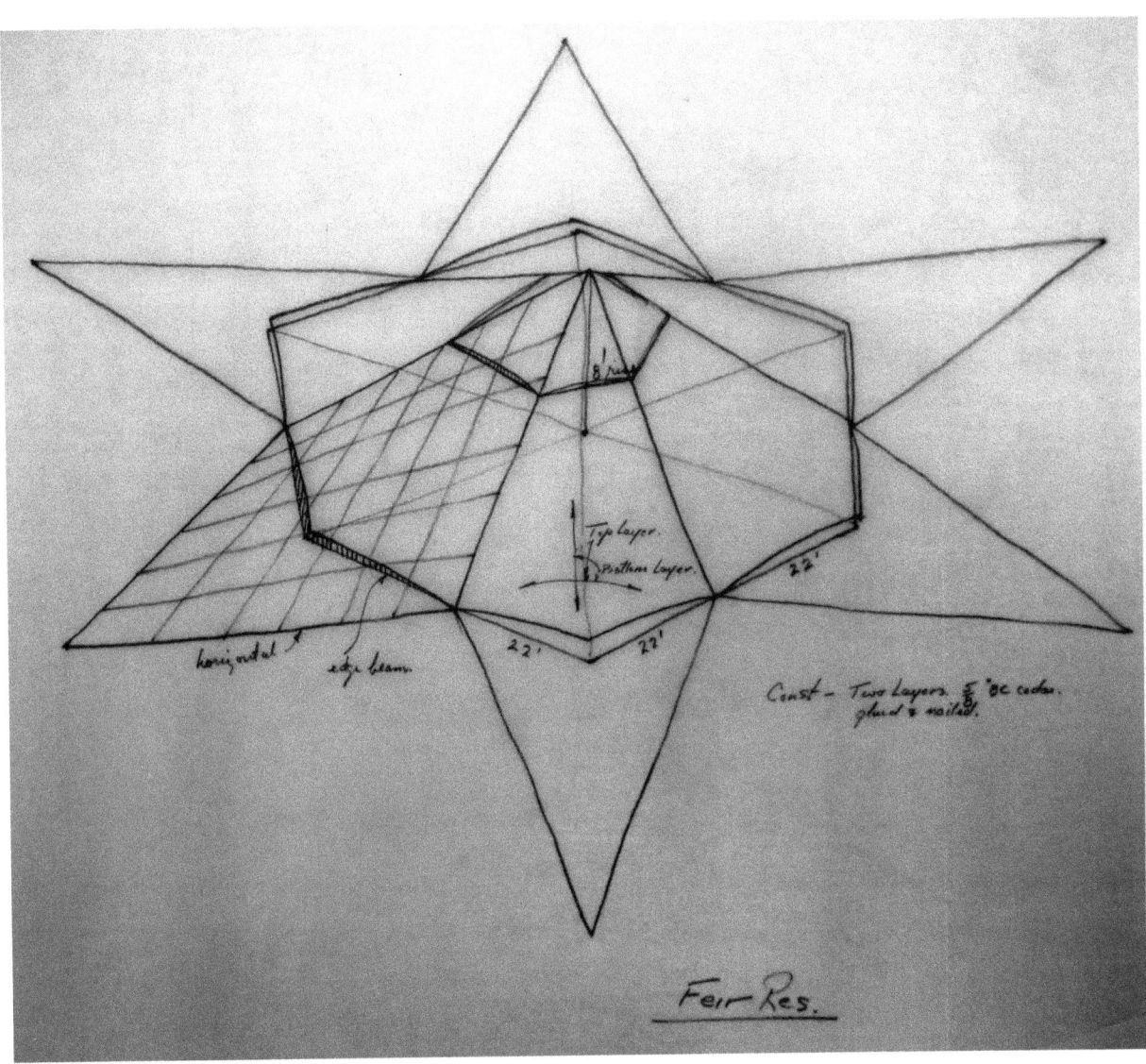

FE house roof concept diagram. "Two Layers. 5/8 BC cedar glued and nailed".
Note crossing Top and Bottom Layers. Max 22' span. Hatched grid is for
illustration purposes only to show angles. (c) JWS 1958

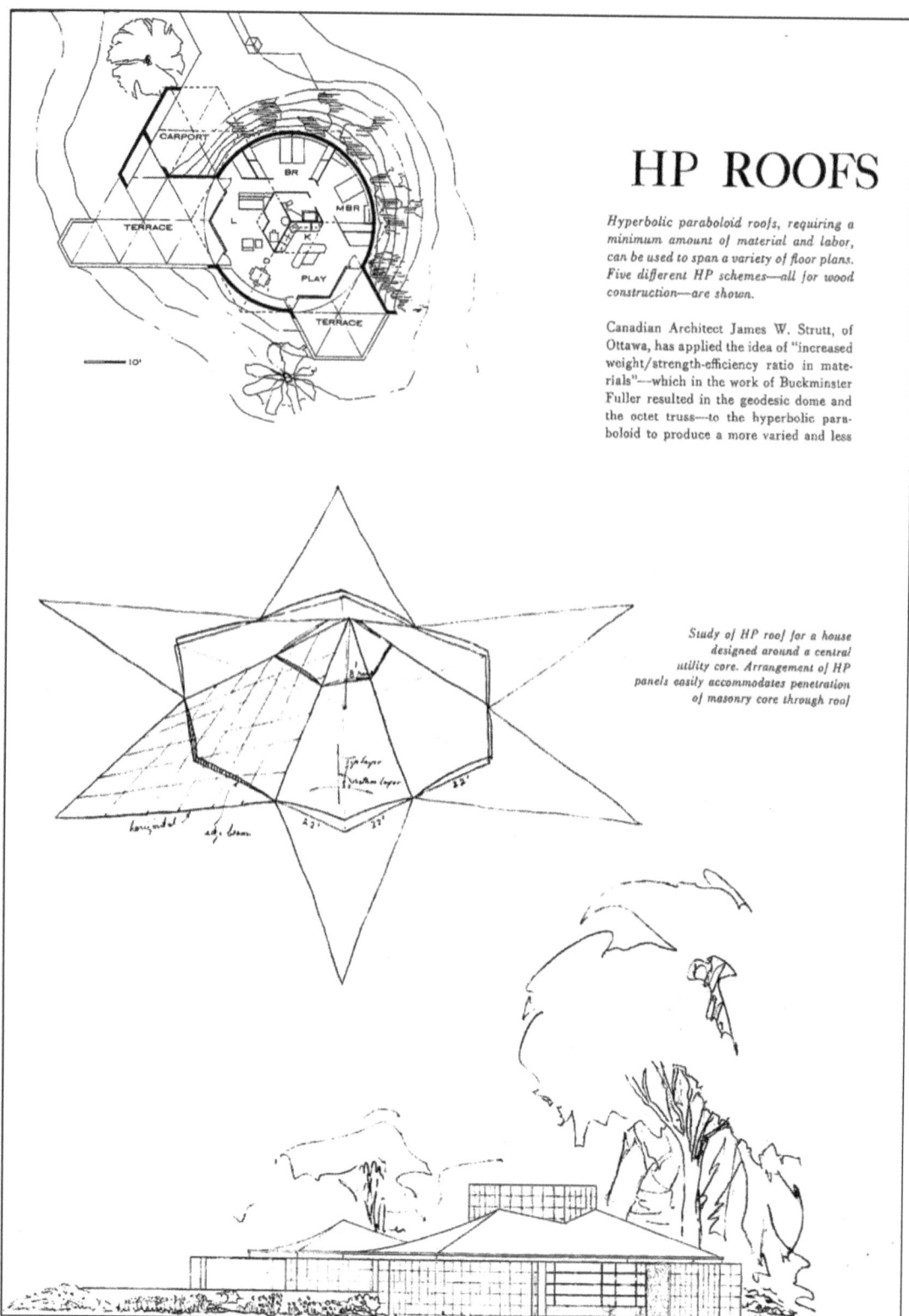

HP ROOFS

Hyperbolic paraboloid roofs, requiring a minimum amount of material and labor, can be used to span a variety of floor plans. Five different HP schemes—all for wood construction—are shown.

Canadian Architect James W. Strutt, of Ottawa, has applied the idea of "increased weight/strength-efficiency ratio in materials"—which in the work of Buckminster Fuller resulted in the geodesic dome and the octet truss—to the hyperbolic paraboloid to produce a more varied and less

Study of HP roof for a house designed around a central utility core. Arrangement of HP panels easily accommodates penetration of masonry core through roof

"HP Roofs for Houses" Progressive Architecture 42-8-113. 1961 p134
https://usmodernist.org/PA/PA-1961-08.pdf

FOR HOUSES

sophisticated roof-construction method. Using only standard materials and methods, he has not only reduced the amount of material required for a given span, but also the amount of labor needed to place it. As the geometry of the HP became familiar, along with the forces within its form, combinations of HP's were evolved so that various applications could be made. In more than twelve of his house designs—four examples are illustrated by sketches—the discipline of the HP's basic geometry, which tends to symmetry and/or

cell-like construction, was the fundamental consideration governing the desirability of its use. The majority of Strutt's applications have been with laminated wood; spans under 30 ft have proved to be most economical, since only two laminations were necessary. In all cases, the cost, including rigid insulation and roofing was below $1.00 per sq ft—a self-imposed limit in order to compete with normal joist construction.

On the West Coast, Architect Paul Hayden Kirk has used HP's for the roof of a

wood-products research home at Bellevue, Washington (SELECTED DETAIL). Of special interest are: the method by which the roof panels are given their doubly-curved form; the simplicity of the roof-drainage system afforded by the use of HP's; and the penetration of one panel by the chimney. This home was a project of the Basic Materials Research and Design Program organized by *Living for Young Homemakers* in co-operation with the Weyerhaeuser Company of St. Paul, Minn., and the Anderson Corp. of Bayport, Minn.

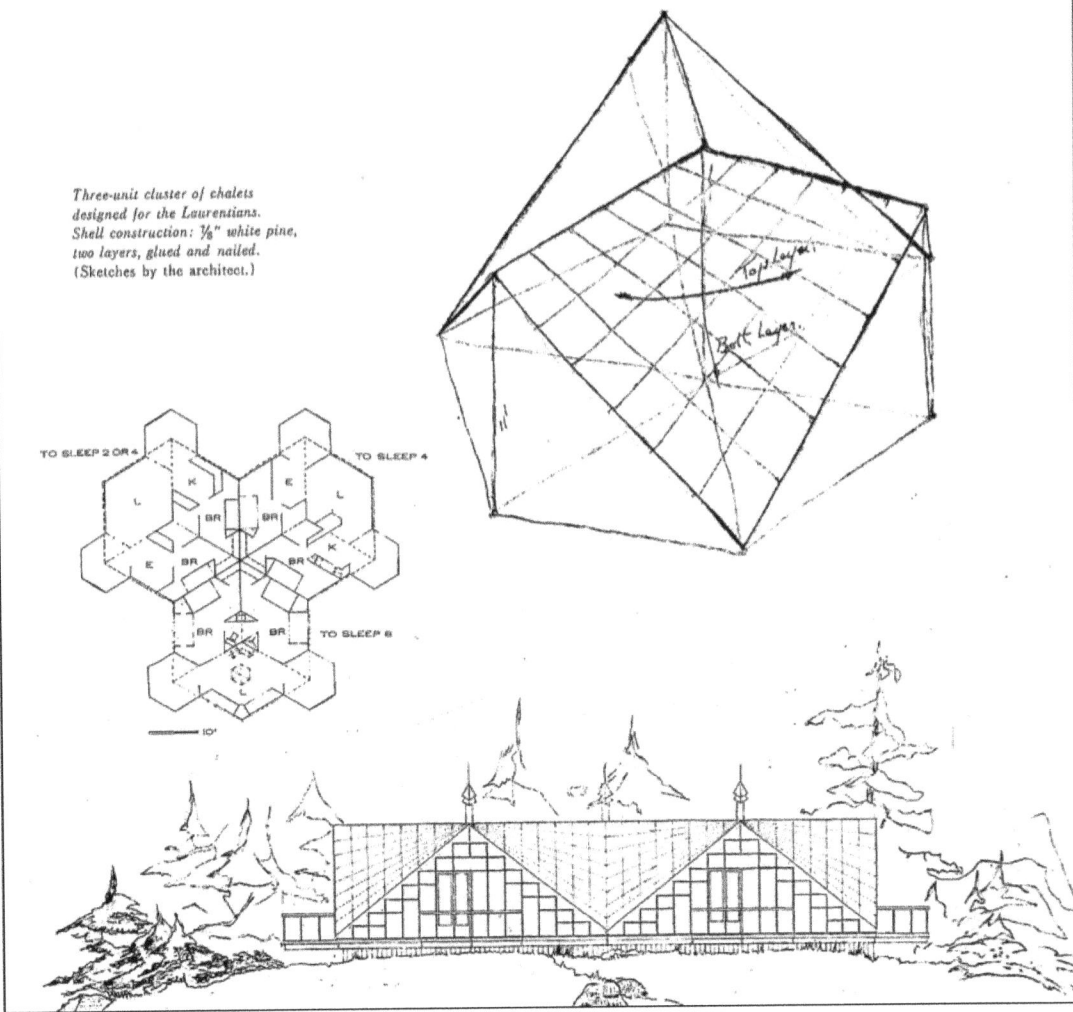

Three-unit cluster of chalets designed for the Laurentians. Shell construction: ⅛" white pine, two layers, glued and nailed. (Sketches by the architect.)

"HP Roofs for Houses" Progressive Architecture 42-8-114. 1961 p135.
https://usmodernist.org/PA/PA-1961-08.pdf

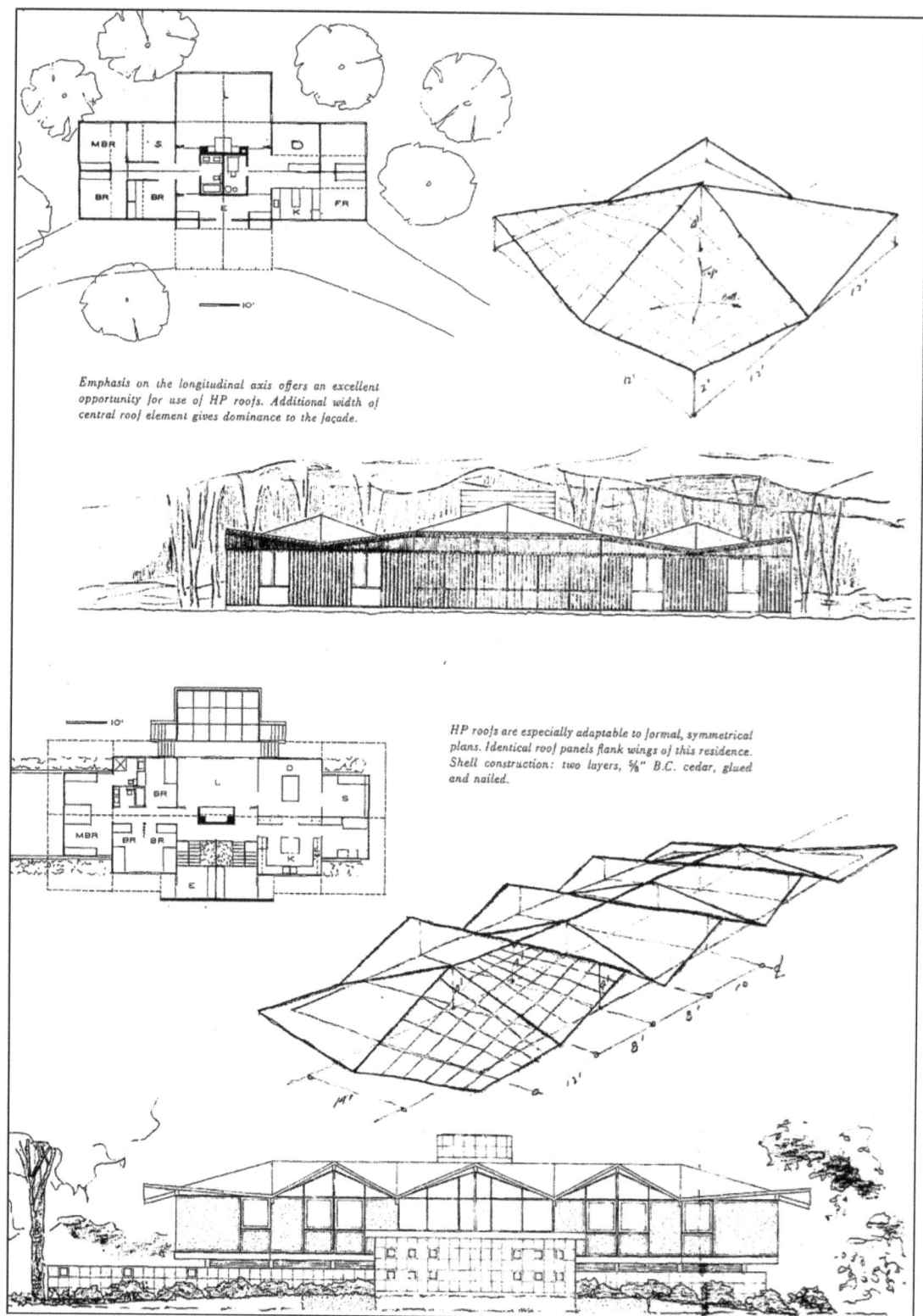

Emphasis on the longitudinal axis offers an excellent
opportunity for use of HP roofs. Additional width of
central roof element gives dominance to the façade.

HP roofs are especially adaptable to formal, symmetrical
plans. Identical roof panels flank wings of this residence.
Shell construction: two layers, ⅝" B.C. cedar, glued
and nailed.

"HP Roofs for Houses" Progressive Architecture 42-8-115. 1961 p136.
https://usmodernist.org/PA/PA-1961-08.pdf

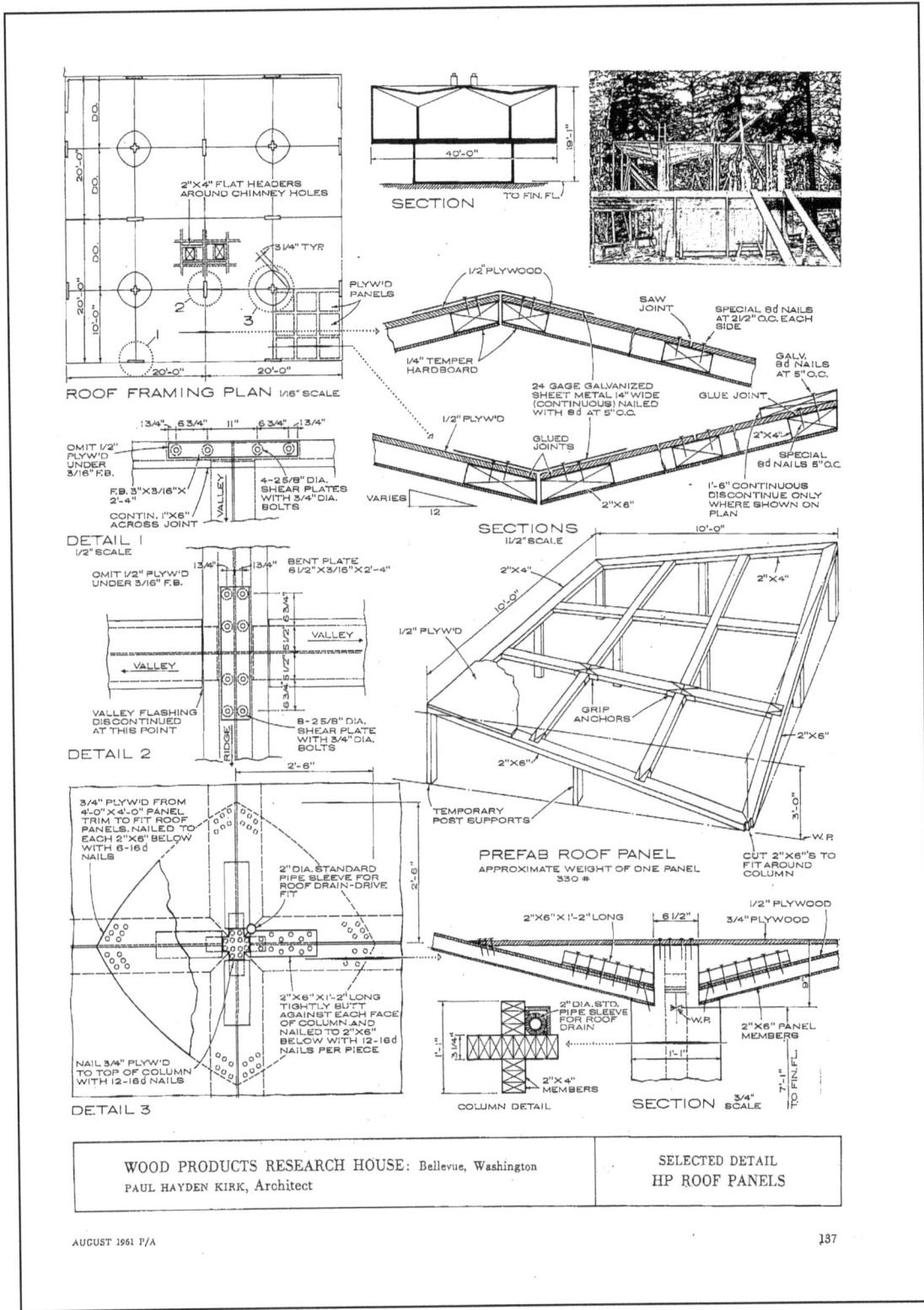

ROOF FRAMING PLAN 1/16" SCALE

2"X4" FLAT HEADERS AROUND CHIMNEY HOLES

PLYW'D PANELS

3 1/4" TYP.

SECTION

TO FIN. FL.

1/2" PLYWOOD

SAW JOINT

SPECIAL 8d NAILS AT 2 1/2" O.C. EACH SIDE

1/4" TEMPER HARDBOARD

GALV. 8d NAILS AT 5" O.C.

24 GAGE GALVANIZED SHEET METAL 14" WIDE (CONTINUOUS) NAILED WITH 8d AT 5" O.C.

GLUE JOINT

1/2" PLYW'D

GLUED JOINTS

2"X4"

SPECIAL 8d NAILS 5" O.C.

VARIES 12

2"X6"

1'-6" CONTINUOUS DISCONTINUE ONLY WHERE SHOWN ON PLAN

SECTIONS 1 1/2" SCALE

DETAIL 1 1/2" SCALE

OMIT 1/2" PLYW'D UNDER 3/16" F.B.

13/4" 63/4" 11" 63/4" 13/4"

F.B. 3"X3/16"X 2'-4"

4-2 5/8" DIA. SHEAR PLATES WITH 3/4" DIA. BOLTS

CONTIN. 1"X6" ACROSS JOINT

VALLEY

DETAIL 2

OMIT 1/2" PLYW'D UNDER 3/16" F.B.

13/4" 13/4"

BENT PLATE 6 1/2"X3/16"X2'-4"

6 3/4" 5 1/2" 6 3/4"

VALLEY

VALLEY

VALLEY FLASHING DISCONTINUED AT THIS POINT

RIDGE

8-2 5/8" DIA. SHEAR PLATE WITH 3/4" DIA. BOLTS

2'-6"

PREFAB ROOF PANEL
APPROXIMATE WEIGHT OF ONE PANEL 330 #

10'-0"

2"X4"

2"X4"

10'-0"

1/2" PLYW'D

GRIP ANCHORS

2"X6"

2"X6"

2"X6"

3'-0"

W.P.

TEMPORARY POST SUPPORTS

CUT 2"X6"'S TO FIT AROUND COLUMN

DETAIL 3

3/4" PLYW'D FROM 4'-0"X 4'-0" PANEL TRIM TO FIT ROOF PANELS. NAILED TO EACH 2"X6" BELOW WITH 6-16d NAILS

2" DIA. STANDARD PIPE SLEEVE FOR ROOF DRAIN-DRIVE FIT

2'-6"

2"X6"X1'-2" LONG TIGHTLY BUTT AGAINST EACH FACE OF COLUMN AND NAILED TO 2"X6" BELOW WITH 12-16d NAILS PER PIECE

NAIL 3/4" PLYW'D TO TOP OF COLUMN WITH 12-16d NAILS

2"X6"X1'-2" LONG

6 1/2"

1/2" PLYWOOD

3/4" PLYWOOD

2" DIA. STD. PIPE SLEEVE FOR ROOF DRAIN

W.P.

2"X6" PANEL MEMBERS

COLUMN DETAIL

2"X4" MEMBERS

3 1/4"

1'-1"

1'-1"

SECTION 3/4" SCALE

7'-1" TO FIN. FL.

| WOOD PRODUCTS RESEARCH HOUSE: Bellevue, Washington | SELECTED DETAIL |
| PAUL HAYDEN KIRK, Architect | HP ROOF PANELS |

AUGUST 1961 P/A

137

"HP Roofs for Houses" Progressive Architecture 42-8-116. 1961 p137.
https://usmodernist.org/PA/PA-1961-08.pdf

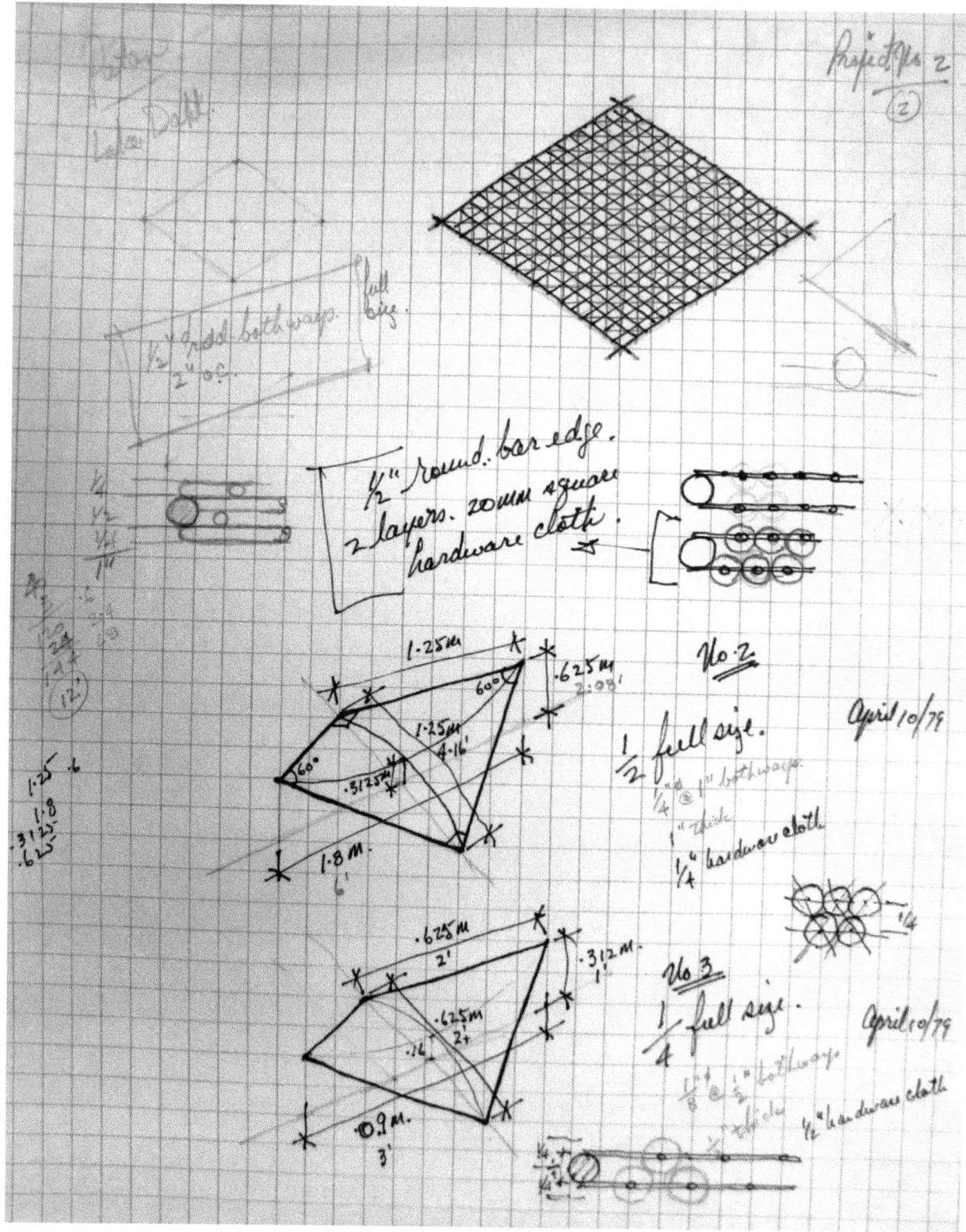

"Rigid Joint Development for polyhedral housing." (c) JWS

In his scheme to achieve a "low-cost house of 1000 sq. ft." the HP roof was a key element since it used minimum materials and had minimum weight.

In the round houses he used two laminated and nailed crosswise layers of cedar boards (or Douglas Fir or unspecified); on the plans for different houses this varies as being 1x4s, 2x4s, 5/8" boards or 3/4" boards. In the G house this was 1x6 T&G western red cedar. The purpose was to have one layer curve in one direction from one side of a section to the other and the second layer cross more-or-less perpendicularly to curve in the other direction. A curved nailing piece served as a template for construction. See the nailing piece diagram. This was a more efficient use of materials than in a conventional bungalow with an attic while at the same time giving a beautiful look on the interior without the need of a finishing layer.

The roof formed a large tent-like structure which was about 14' high where it met the block wall of the inside central core sloping down to about 7' at the exterior wall where it extended a few feet beyond the block wall to form an eve overhang with recessed lighting. In the bedrooms the roof similarly was high towards the centre and low at the exterior wall where there was also an overhang with lighting.

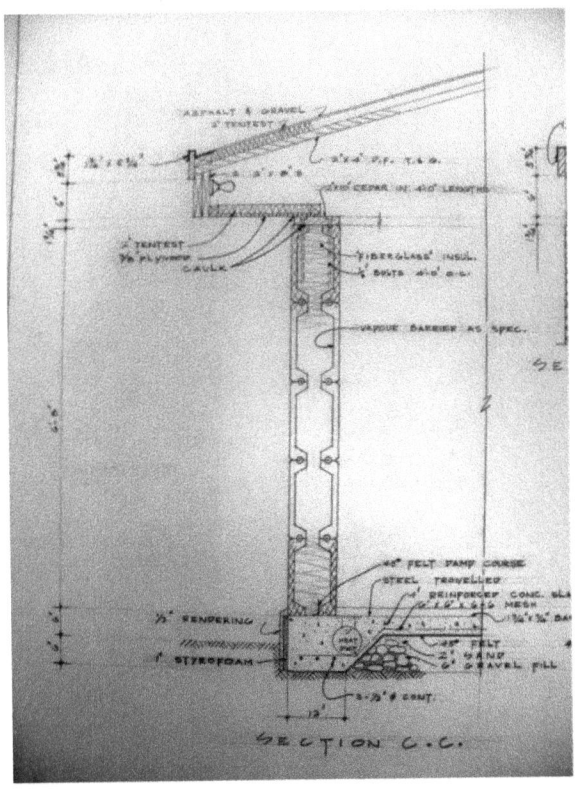

P house exterior wall section at roof. The roof has "2 inch tentest over 2x4 D.F. [Douglas fir] T&G". Note recessed lighting. Note five rows of 4"x16"x16" blocks. (c) JWS 1959.

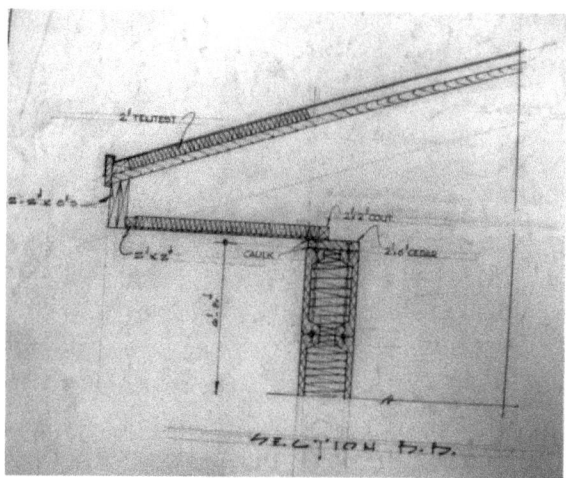

FE house and typical, roof section B-B top of exterior wall. The roof has "2 inch tentest". (c) JWS 1958

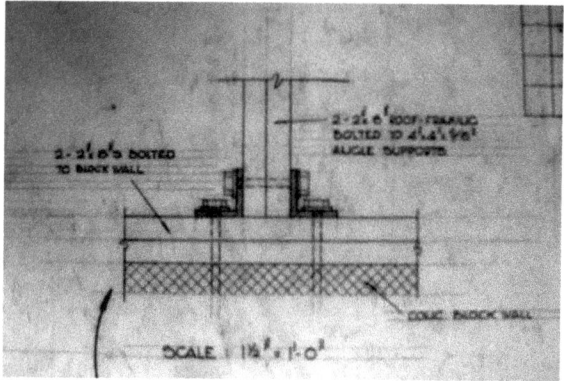

FE house roof beam connection to the top of the central block wall on the flat. (c) JWS 1958

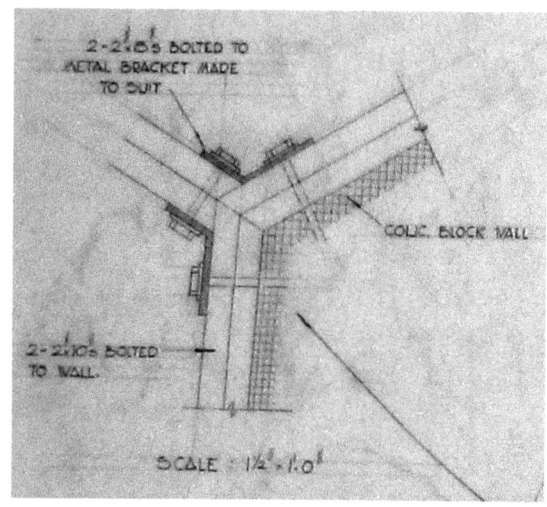

Roof beam attachment (c) JWS

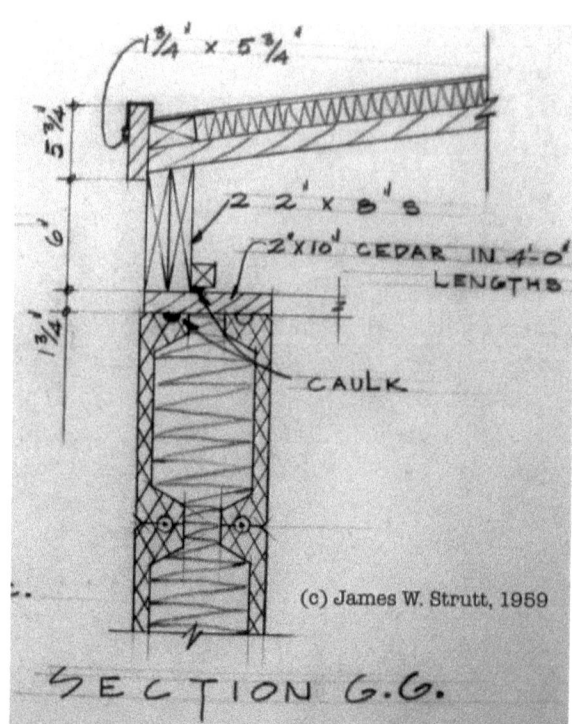

P house exterior block wall and roof interface. Note the lack of overhang. (c) JWS

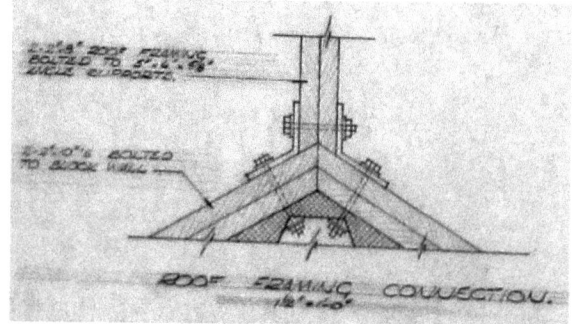

G house "Roof Framing connection" to the top of central block wall at the corner. Detail. (c) JWS

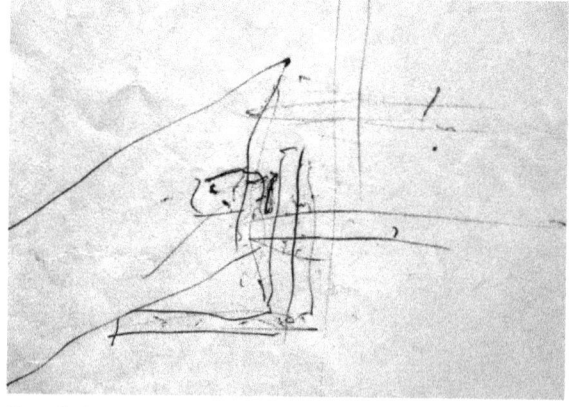

Roof beam marginalia. (c) JWS

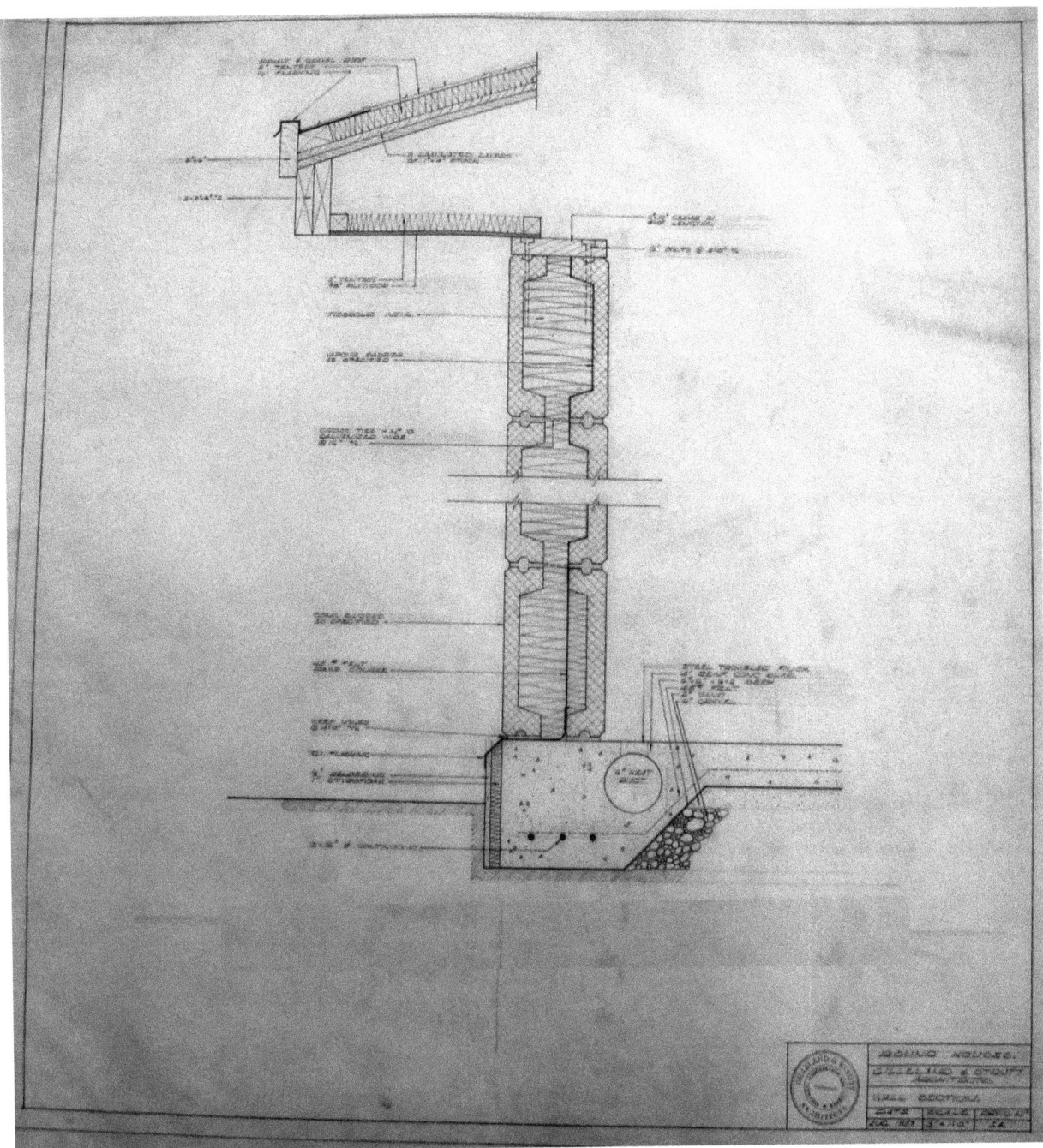

Round houses typical wall section, roof support. The roof has "2 inch
tentest over 2 laminated layers of 1x4 stock".

Note 4"x16"x16" blocks with a cavity for Fiberglas insulation; compare this
with the section drawing in the Block walls chapter which has 4"x8"x16"
blocks, page 52. The latter is what was actually used.

(c) JWS August 1959

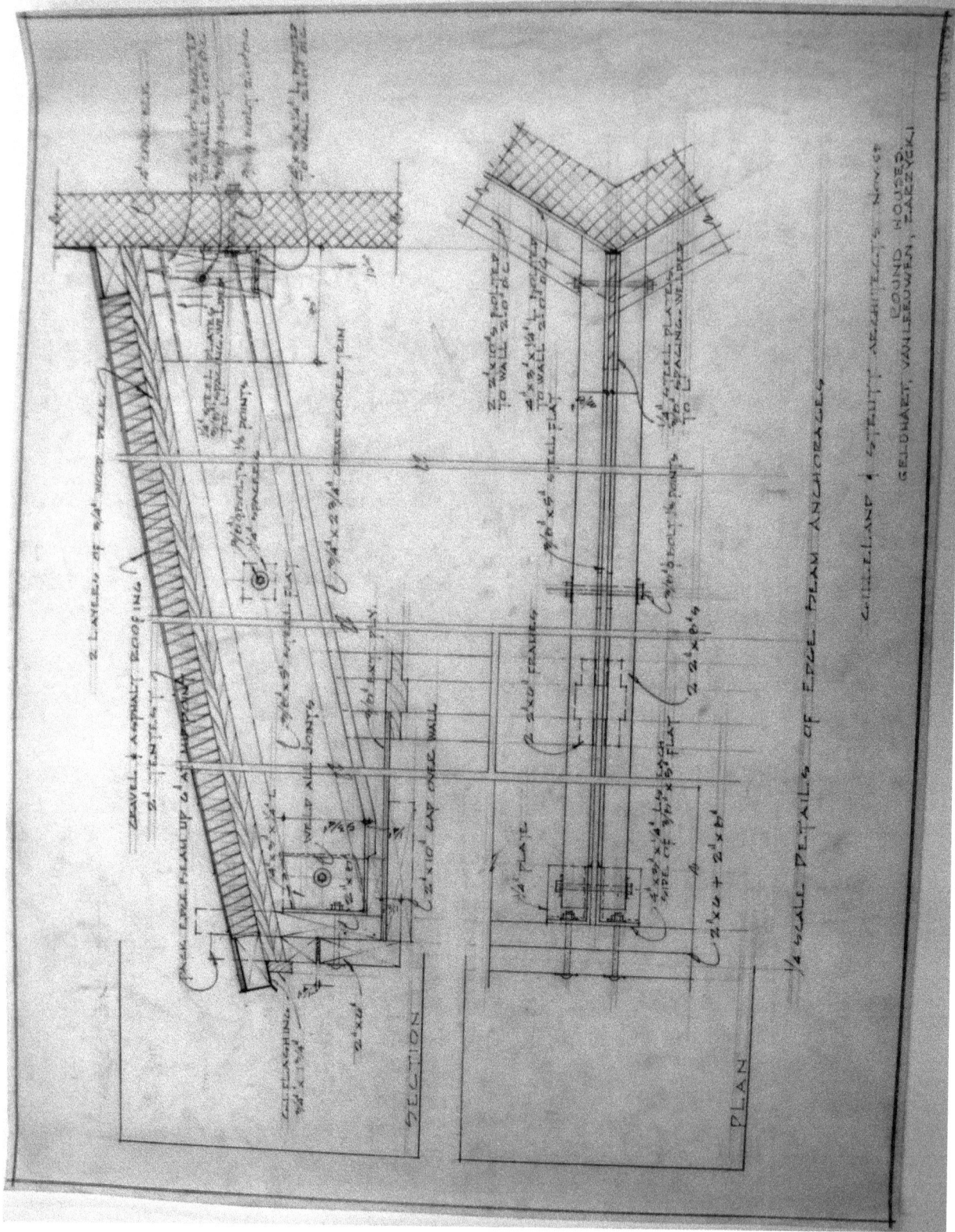

G, V, and Z houses. "Details of Edge Beam Anchorages" to the top of the block walls at a corner of the central hexagon. The roof has "2 inch tentest over 2 layers of 3/4" wood deck" (c) JWS 1959.

The round houses are beautiful and would be fine in dry and warm climates but they were not designed for the Canadian winter even though Strutt followed building practices acceptable at the time.

Insulation improvements.

Above the roofing boards was 2" of fibreboard (tentest) insulation covered by asphalt and gravel roofing. These were the days before the energy crisis of the 1970s and fuel was so inexpensive that thick wall and roof insulation was not a priority.

The escape of heat from the interior house tended to melt the snow above allowing the puddling of water and the growth of icicles over the roof edge. Further, where the main curving roof met lower down with the carport or wing room roof, the drainage angle was not sufficient and water puddled, and the roofing material tended to degrade and leak.

In the G house the roof had to be resurfaced about once every ten years and about 1990 a new covering structure with Fiberglas insulation and cold air space was added on top of the existing roof.

Structural improvements.

In the G house, the weight of the winter snow after a couple of years started to cause the connection of the roof beams at the top of the central core block wall to weaken and disconnect, and cause the exterior concrete block supporting walls to lean out off the vertical. The owner, DMG, pointed this out in a letter to the builder in 1963, two winters after construction, quote:

> Under the weight of snow, serious failure has occurred in the support members of the main roof and the three wing roofs. In order to prevent costly damage and to restore the support members to their intended function, it is urgent that the structure be checked without delay.
>
> Already leaks have occurred throughout the house and the supporting walls of the three wings have been forced out of vertical. The most dangerous defect is that the joists for the main roof are pulling away from their anchorage on the central pillar.

The owner had to contract to consultants and a separate welding firm for the design and installation of a remedial steel umbrella to hold the supporting walls to the central core, and tie the roof beams one to the other with steel rods, with tie rods holding the walls of the three wing rooms together. This was done within the building to be as unobtrusive to the living space as possible.

Remedial steel beams in main living
area linked to a steel post (not
shown) in the central hexagon. 1965

Original interior, during
construction. 1960

Remedial steel tie rods, Apartment
wing. 1965

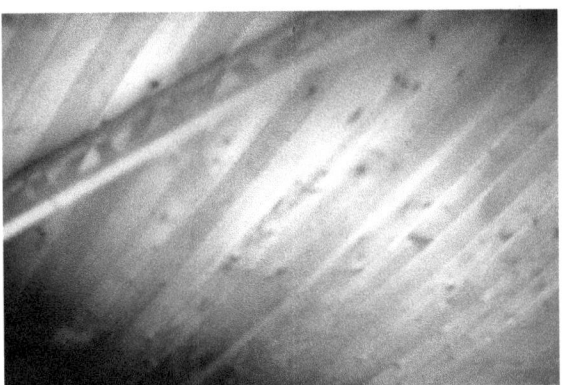

Remedial roof beam, added 1965

G house roof, interior

G house roof construction. Top left, finished with tar. Above shows boards on main roof and temporary framing on wing room (left) and carport (right) 1960.

Windows

The outdoors is always visible from the living-dining area in the round houses because two sets of full-height patio windows face onto terraces. In some houses there is one door in the patio window area and in others two, one on either side. Windows are two panes of D.D. (double diamond brand) glass not thermal pane. The window framing is custom-made ripped cedar.

The bedrooms have one opening window each while the larger master bedroom has two (In the V house the master bedroom has two double windows). These were also framed with cedar to fit, made on site or nearby.

In the round houses there were diamond-shaped skylights above the central core to illuminate the kitchen, bathroom and services room.

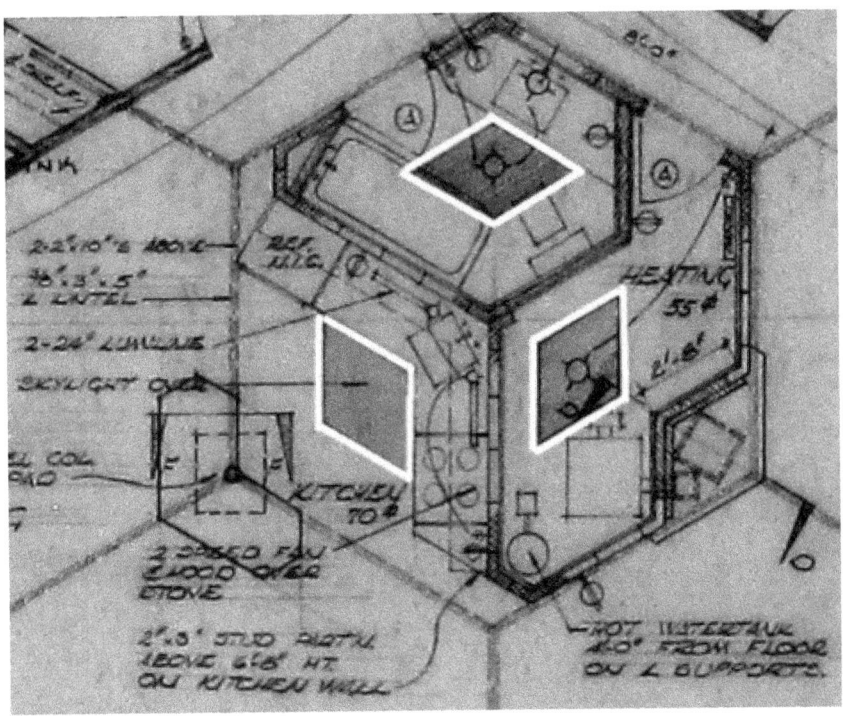

G house Plan detail showing the location of skylights (author's highlighting). (c) JWS

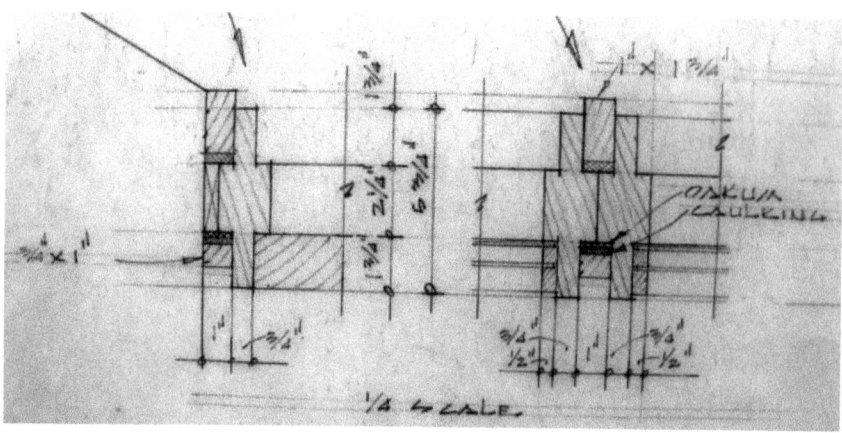

P house patio windows framing A. (c) JWS

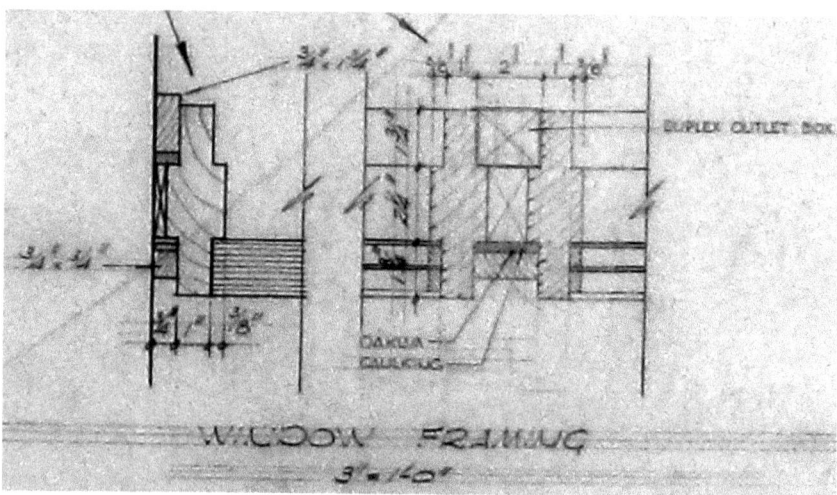

G house patio window framing B. (c) JWS

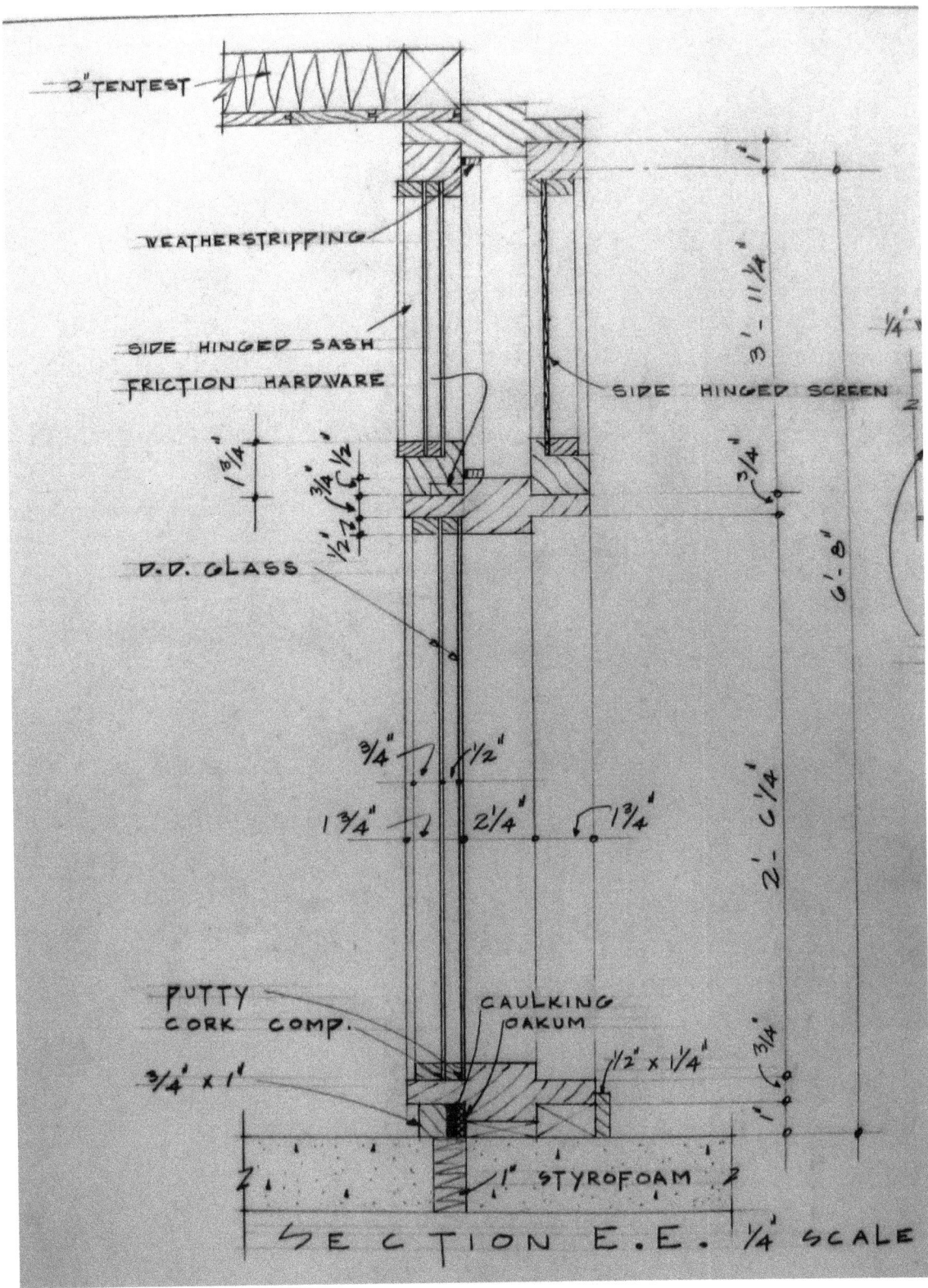

SECTION E.E. 1/4 SCALE

Labels in figure: 2" TENTEST; WEATHERSTRIPPING; SIDE HINGED SASH; FRICTION HARDWARE; SIDE HINGED SCREEN; D.D. GLASS; PUTTY; CORK COMP.; CAULKING; OAKUM; 3/4" x 1"; 1/2" x 1/4"; 1" STYROFOAM

P house. Patio window section. Note vertical dimensions are abbreviated and not to scale but this is not indicated: the upper opening screened window is 3'-11 1/4" and the lower window is 2'- 6 1/4". Other round houses similar. (c) JWS

Working in the west patio window area. 1960

West patio windows. Note remedial steel work at roof (installed 1965). c. 1980

West patio windows detail. Icicles indicate an insufficiently insulated roof. 1961

G house

Lighting

Sockets for incandescent light bulbs were at various locations throughout the house: in the recessed roof overhangs in the living area and in the bedrooms throwing light up onto the cedar T&G roof boards; in simple custom-made triangular boxes with frosted glass bottoms in the hallway, bedrooms and the laundry room; in the overhangs at the patio windows to shed light down through a glass bottom to the outside terraces (in the G house the latter were removed about 1980 when it became necessary to insulate the area).

In the kitchen and bathroom of the main house and in the kitchenette and shower room of the apartment suites were two sets of 16" fluorescent tube lights above the counters.

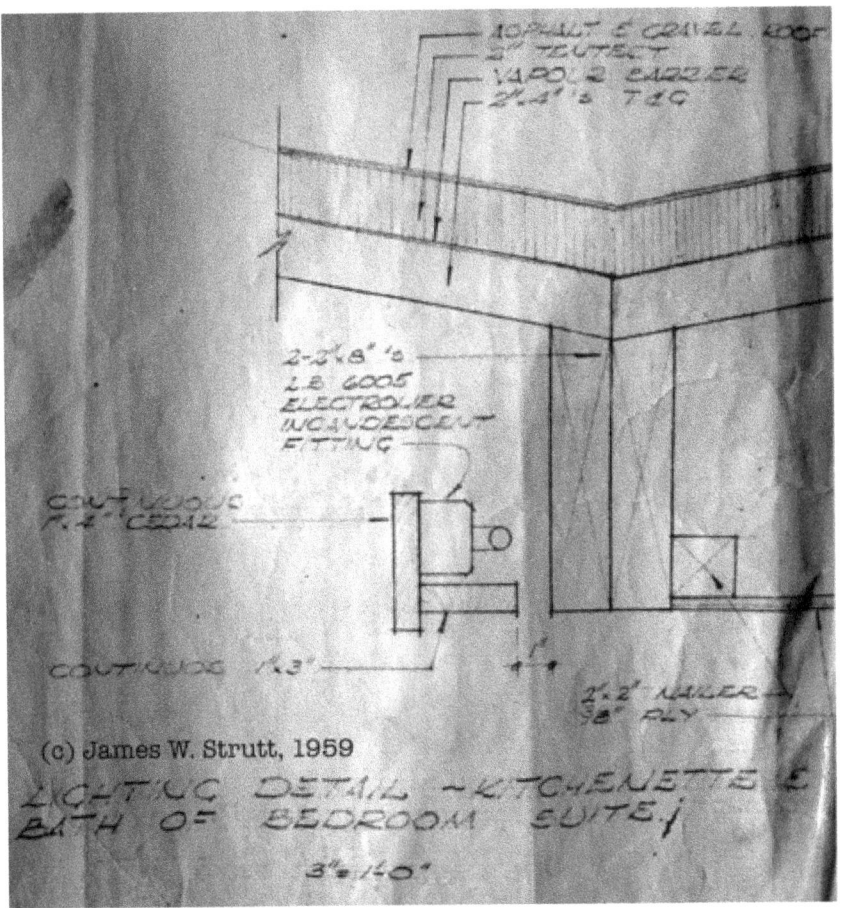

(c) James W. Strutt, 1959

G house fluorescent lighting detail bedroom suite. "Incandescent" should read "fluorescent". Note upper section showing where the main roof and the wing room roof meet. (c) JWS

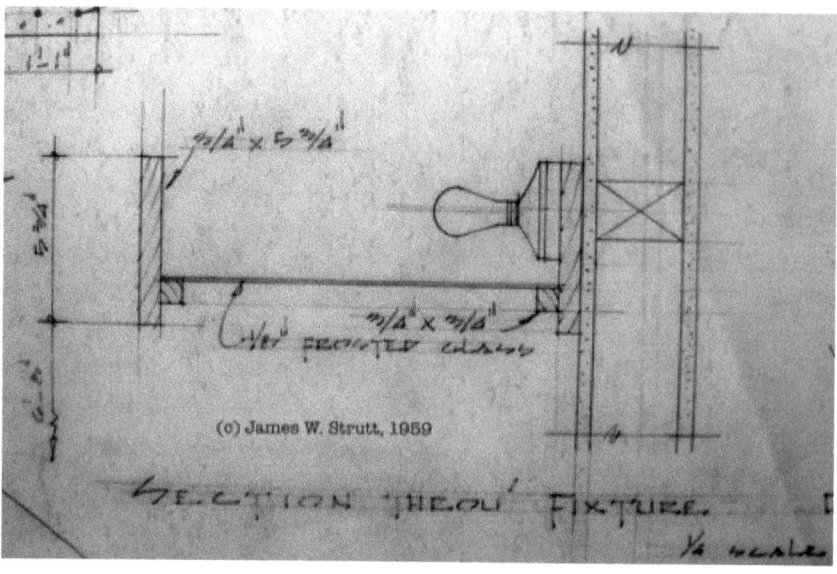

P house overhead light box. Other houses similar.
(c) JWS

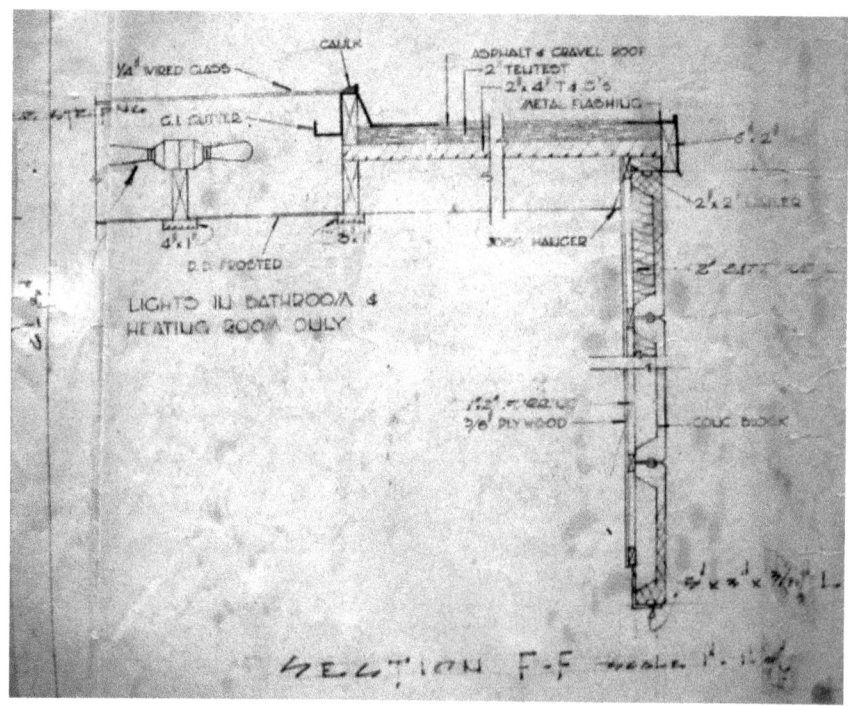

G house hallway lighting section. (c) JWS

Fireplace

In Strutt's conception of the single family home it may have gone without saying that, along with extensive patio windows, there must be a fireplace. In the round houses it was a diamond shaped column in the central block wall facing the living area.

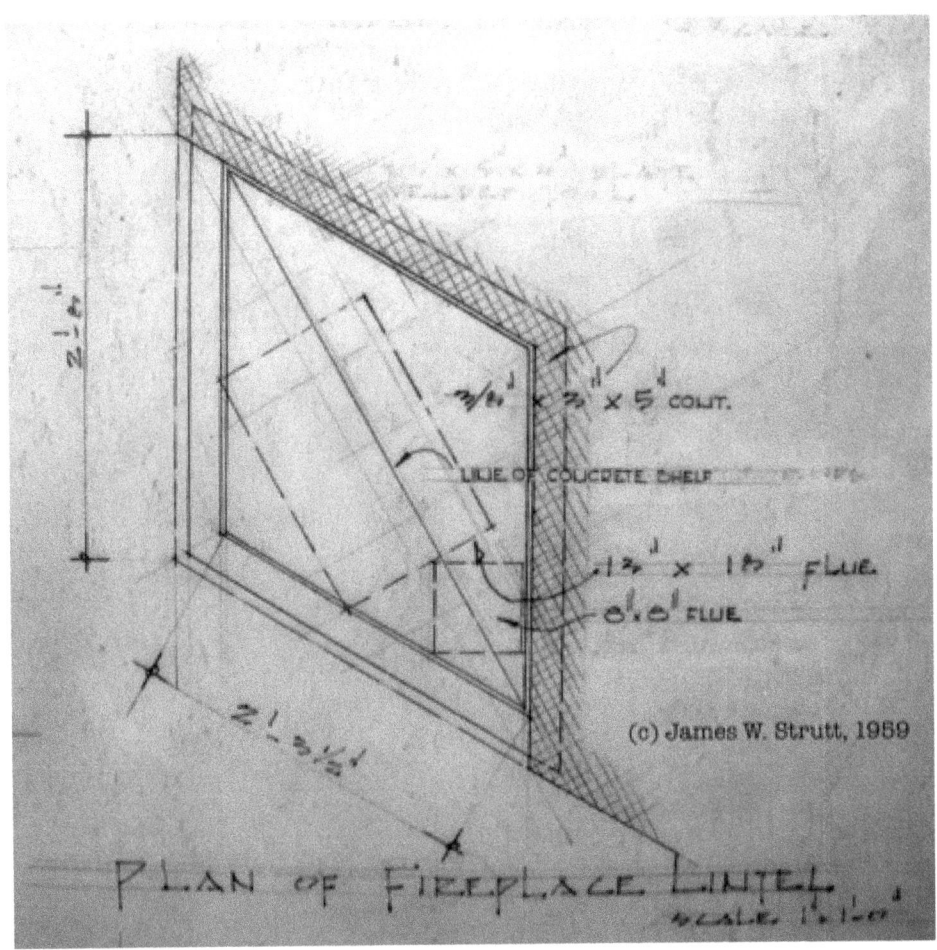

P house fireplace lintel (c) JWS

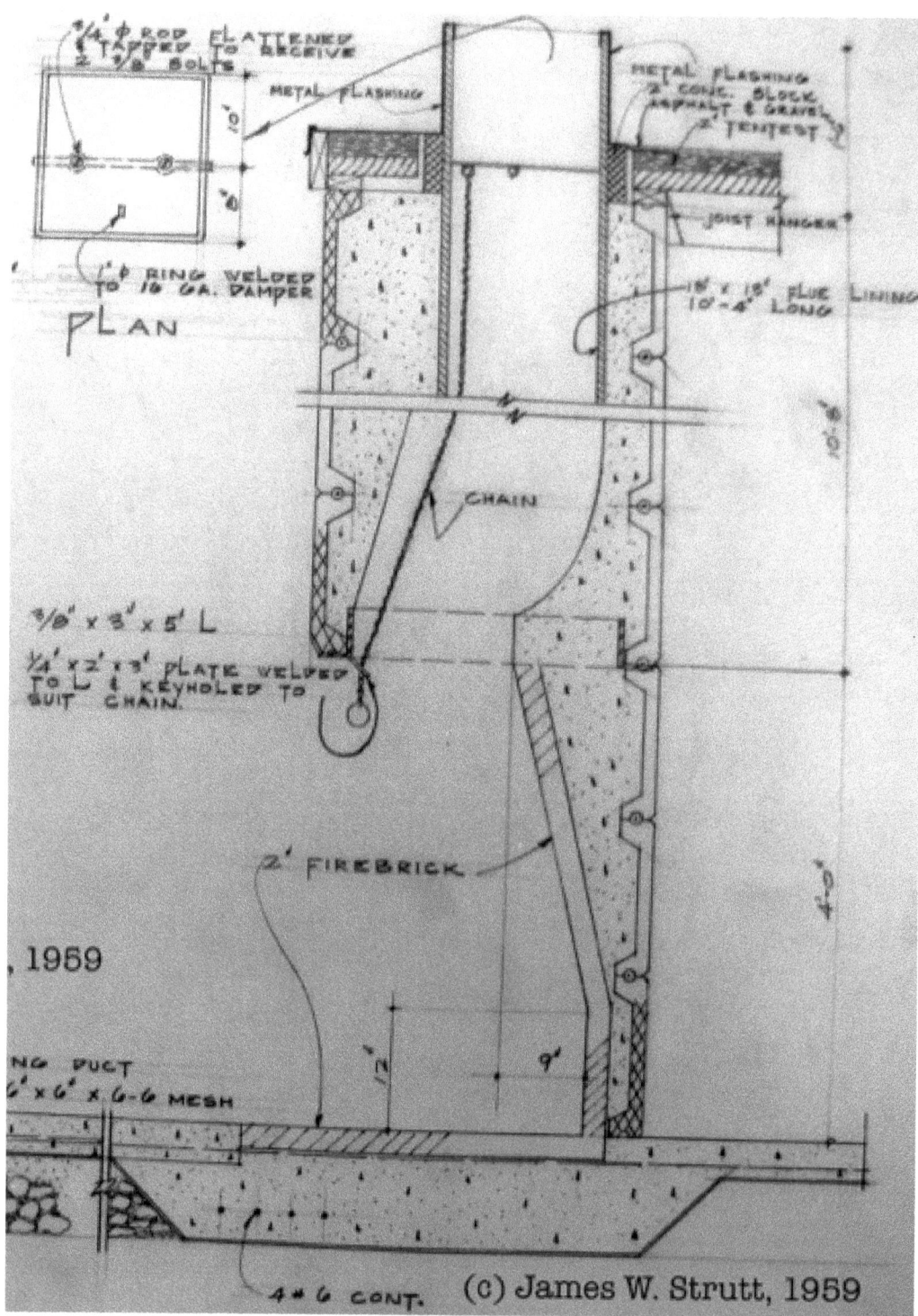

P house Chimney Section (c) JWS

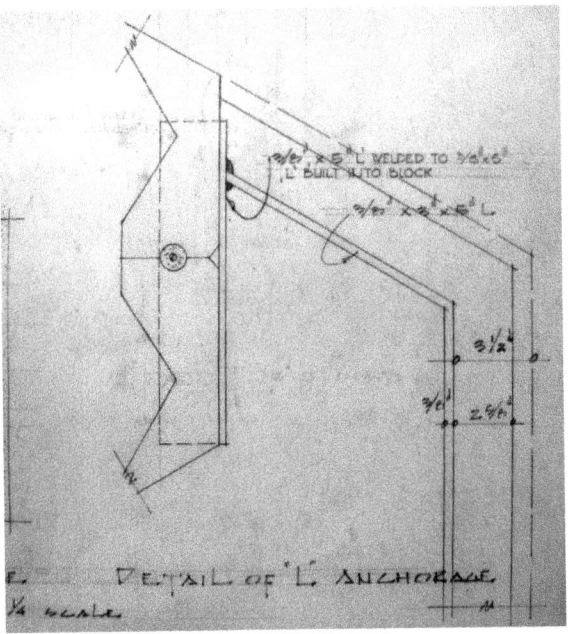

P house fireplace anchorage. (c) JWS

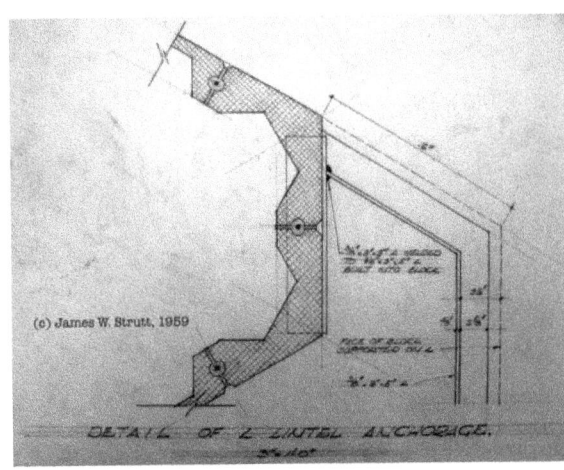

Z house fireplace lintel anchorage (c) JWS

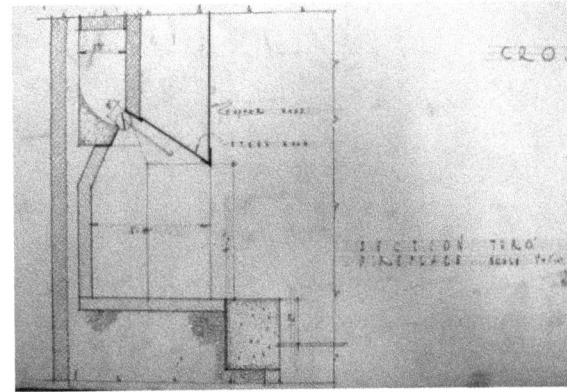

Section through fireplace (c) JWS

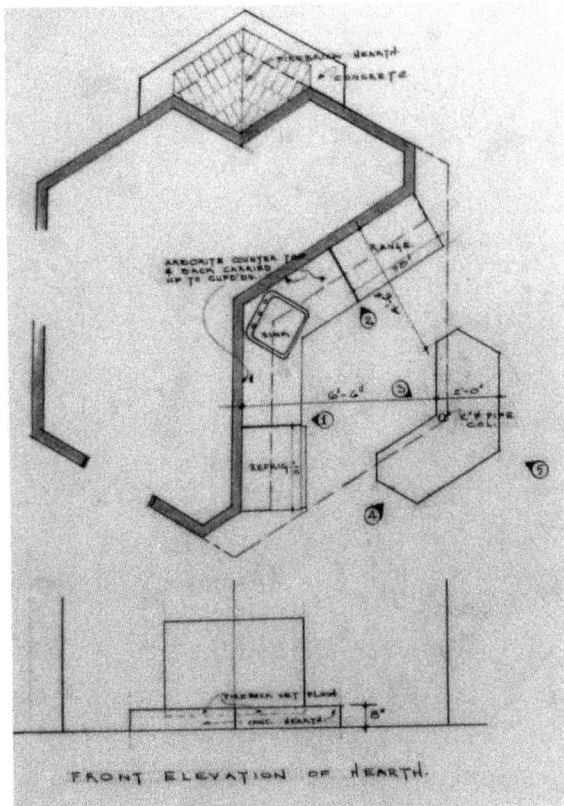

G house hearth in plan (top) and elevation (bottom), with kitchen.

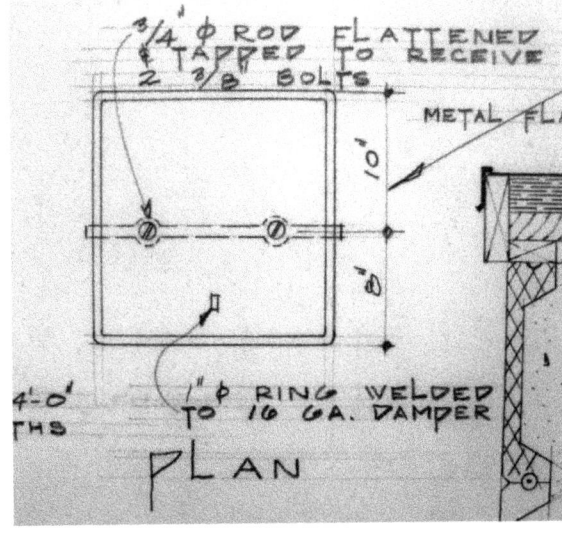

P house chimney flue plan. (c) JWS

Fireplace. c. 1962

Fireplace. c. 1990.

Central block hexagon
showing wood stove and
fireplace. c. 2010

G house

Kitchen

Within the confines of the central hexagon of 8'-long sides at 120°, the kitchen was designed in consultation with the client. Kitchen (and bathrooms and laundry room) cupboards and drawers were custom-made of 5/8" plywood with mahogany laminate. Mahogany nosing was used around the counters. "Lemon-yellow furniture finish" arborite was used for countertop and backing.

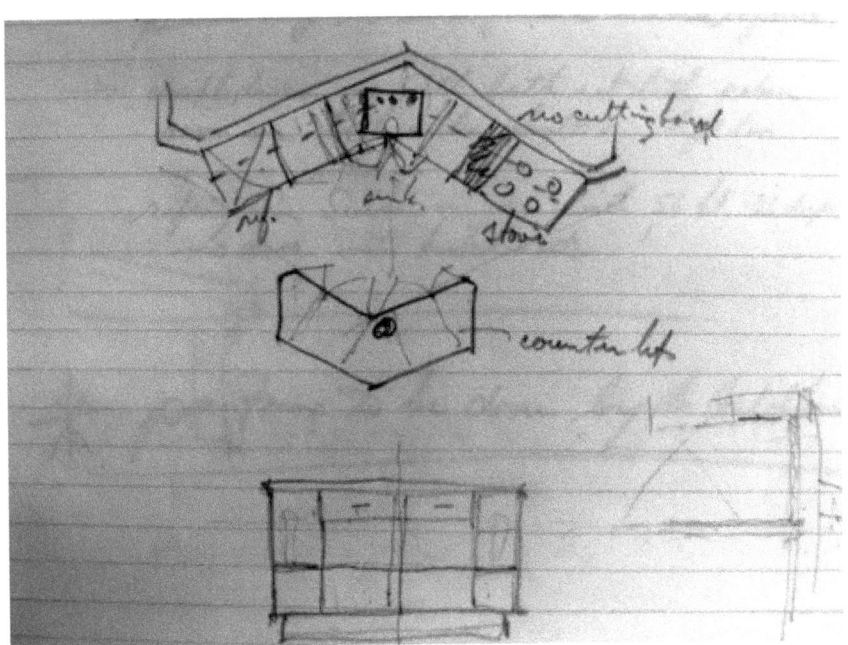

G house kitchen sketch (c) JWS 1960

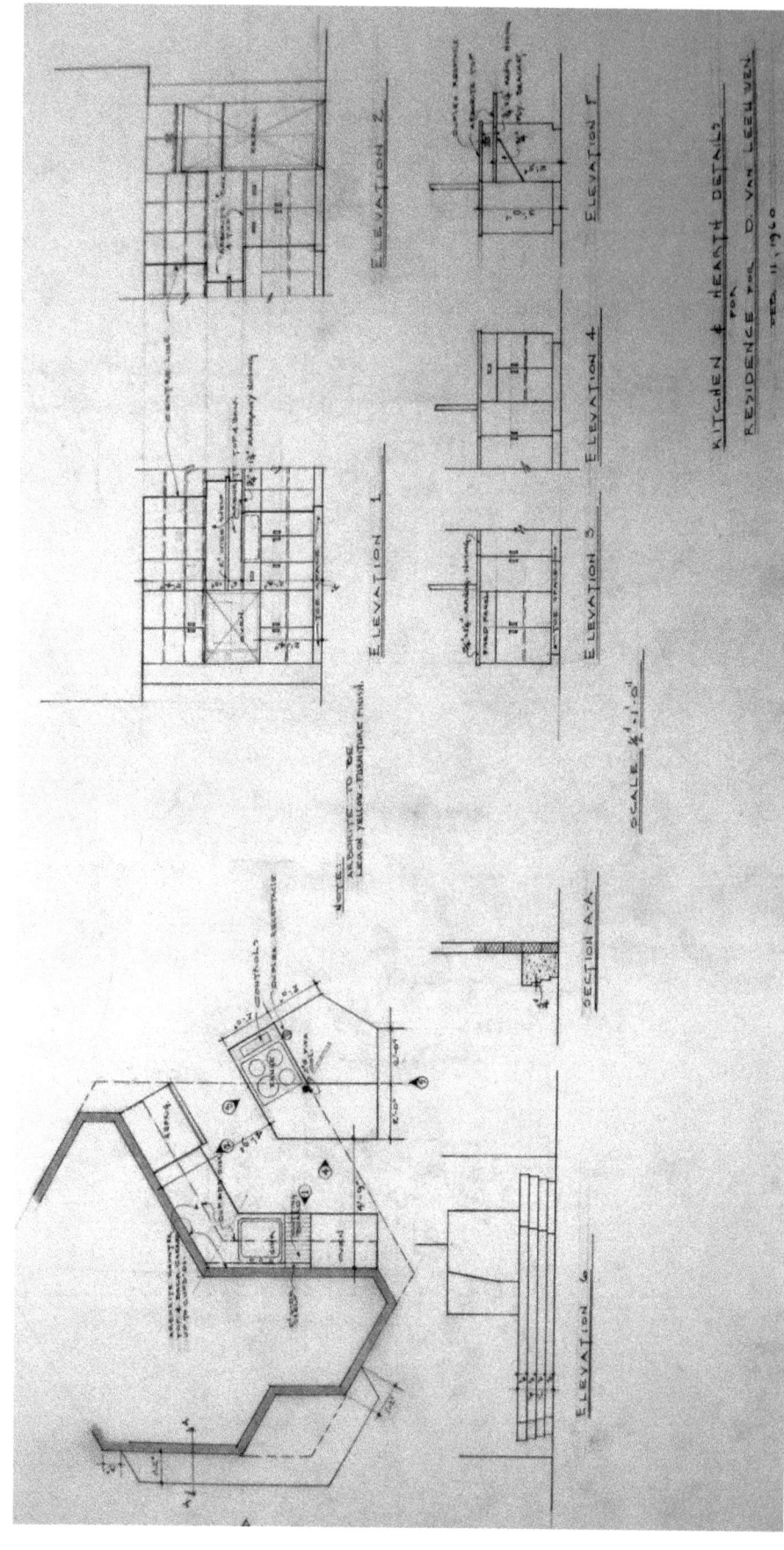

V house. Kitchen. Note the kitchen island follows the angle of the sink counter, and contains the range. The hearth (fireplace) is a diamond shape at the left and its elevation and section are shown below. (c) JWS 1960

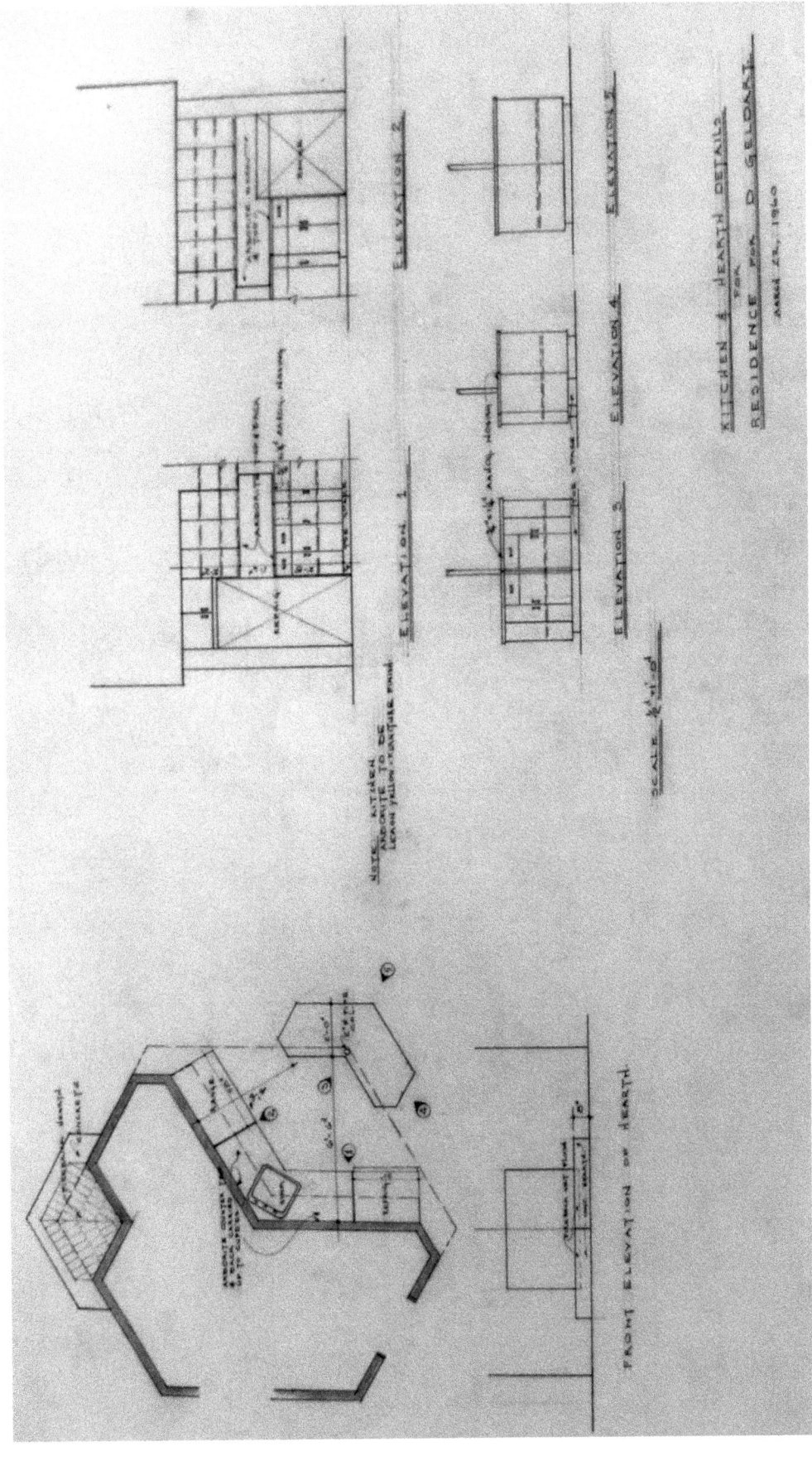

G house kitchen plan and elevations. Notes: island opposes the angle of the sink counter; top: fireplace (hearth) faces the living room. (c) JWS 1960

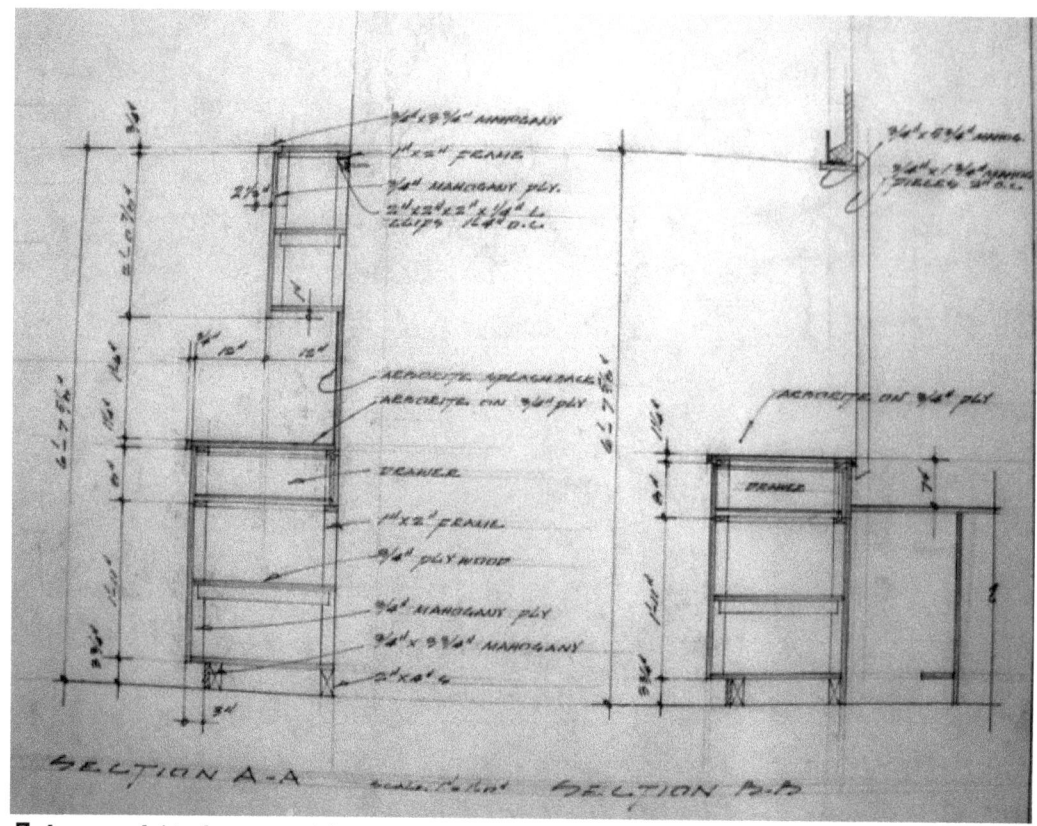

Z house kitchen sections A-A & B-B (c) JWS

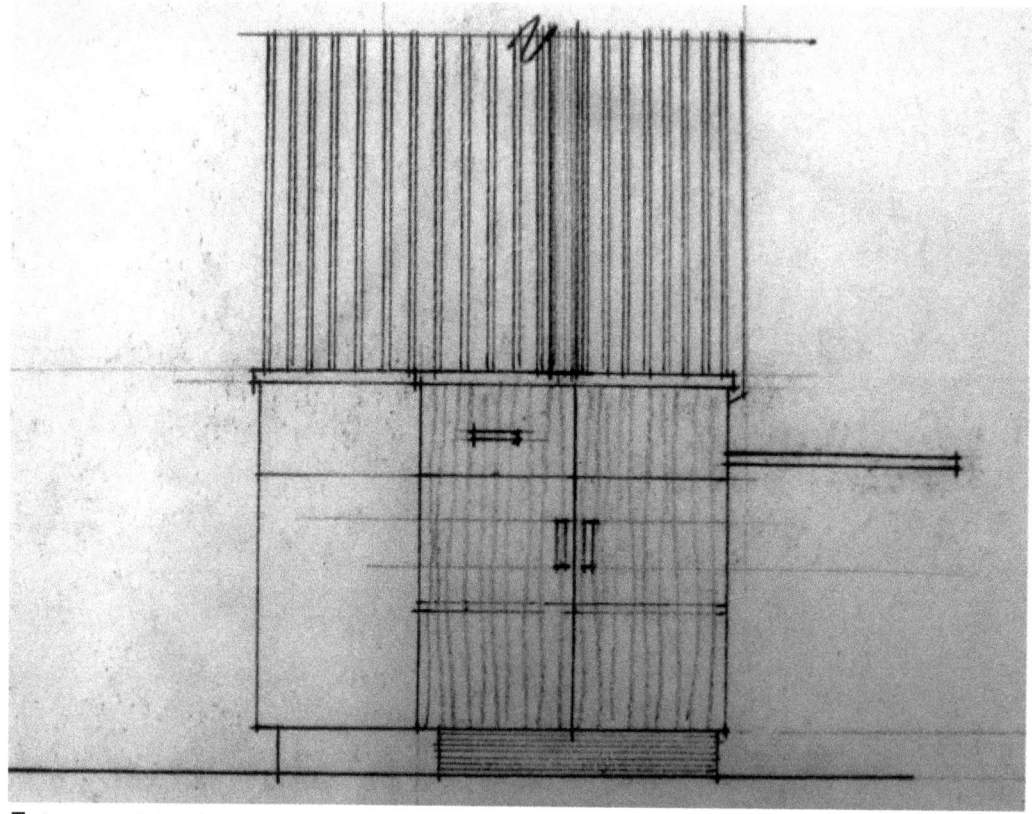

Z house kitchen elevation 3 (c) JWS

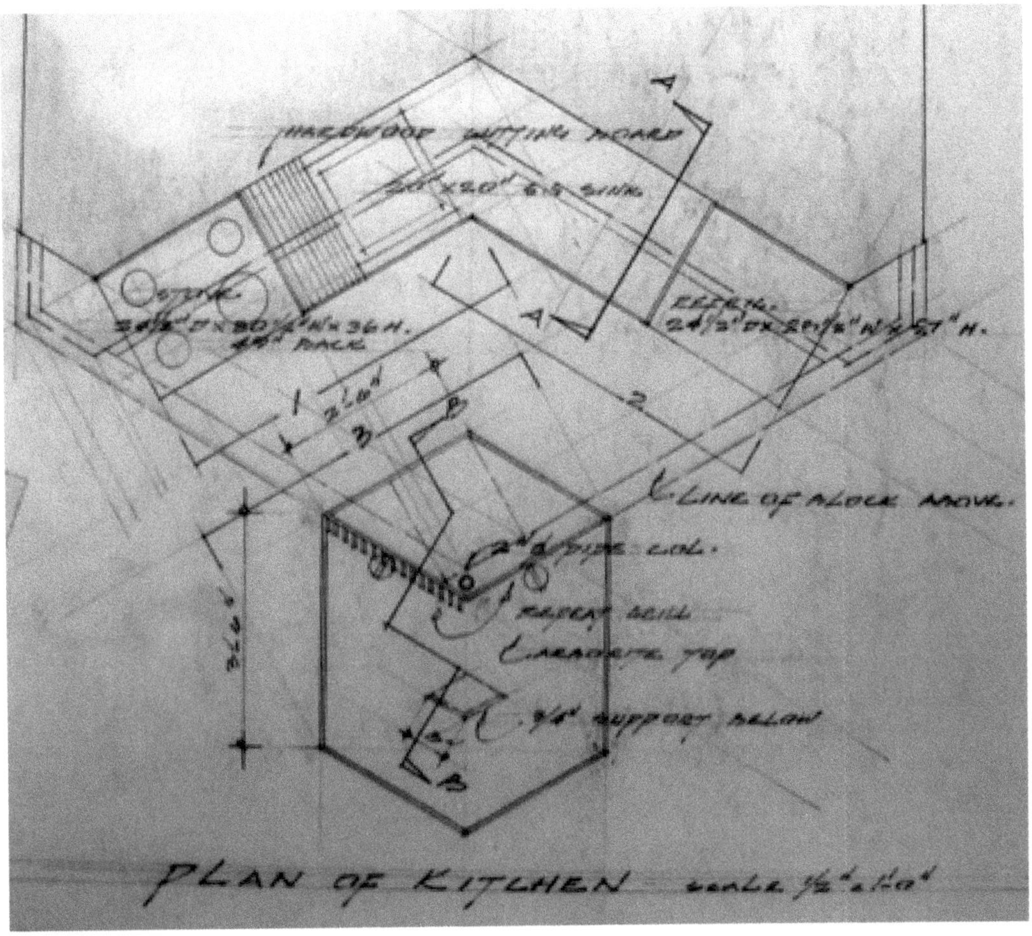

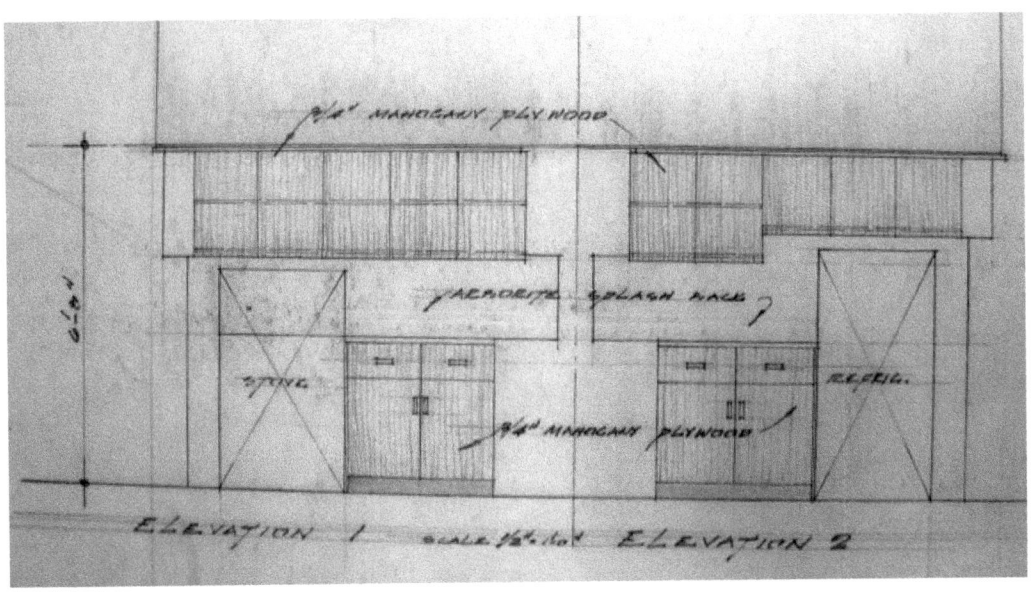

Z house kitchen plan.(c) JWS

Z house kitchen elevations 1 & 2 (c) JWS

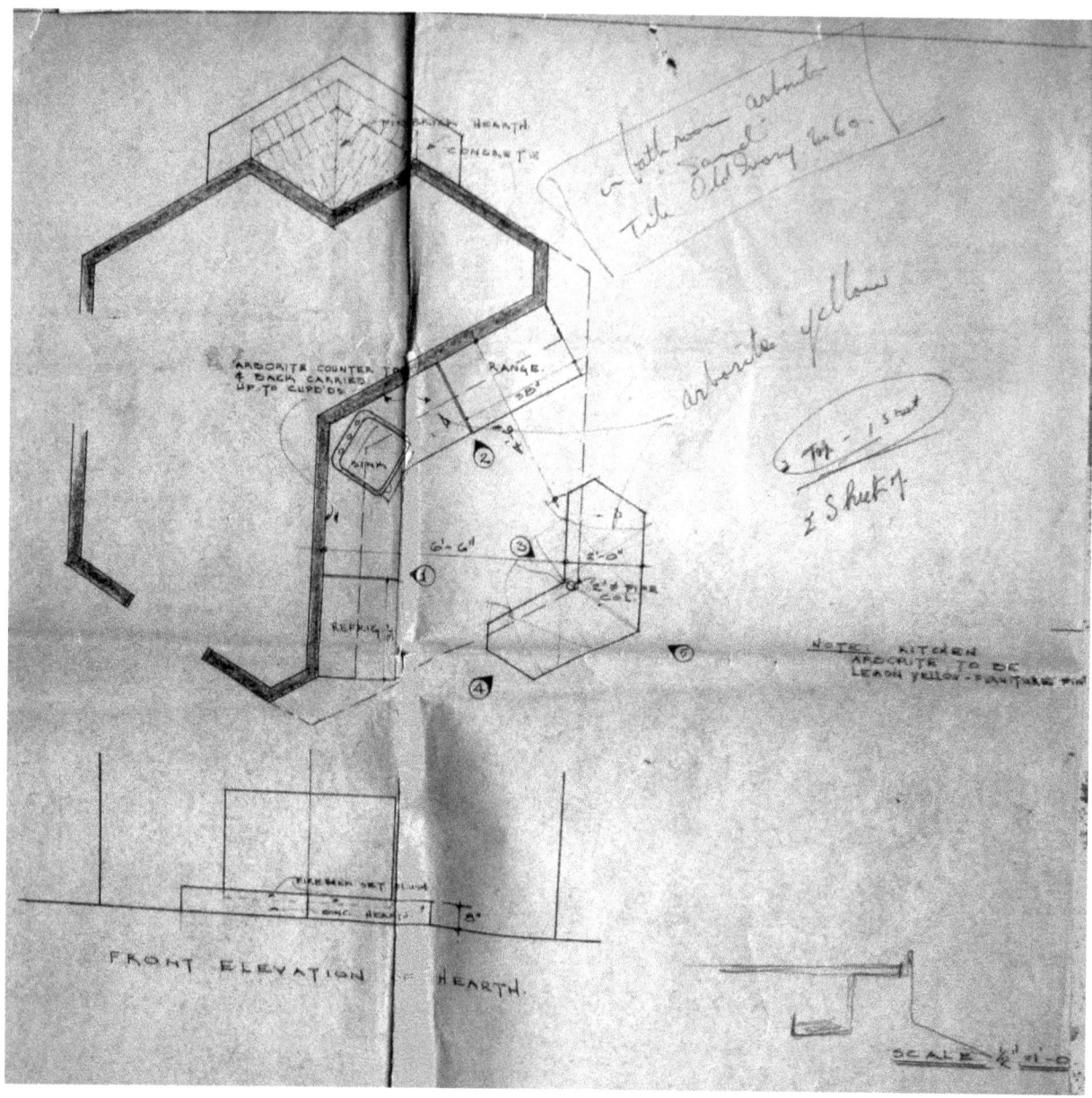

G house kitchen and hearth with notes. (c) JWS 1960

Location of the main kitchen (left) in the central core. De-furnished 2017

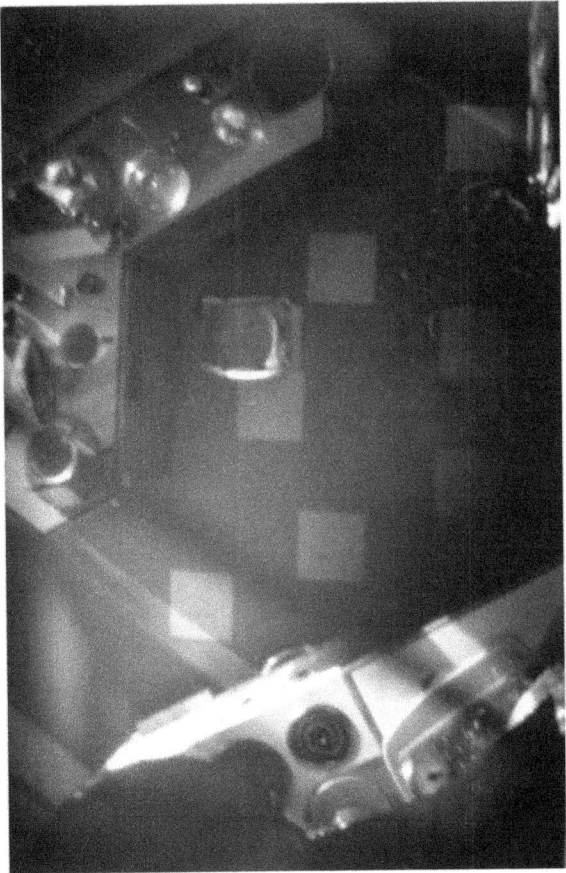

Main kitchen from above. c. 1990.

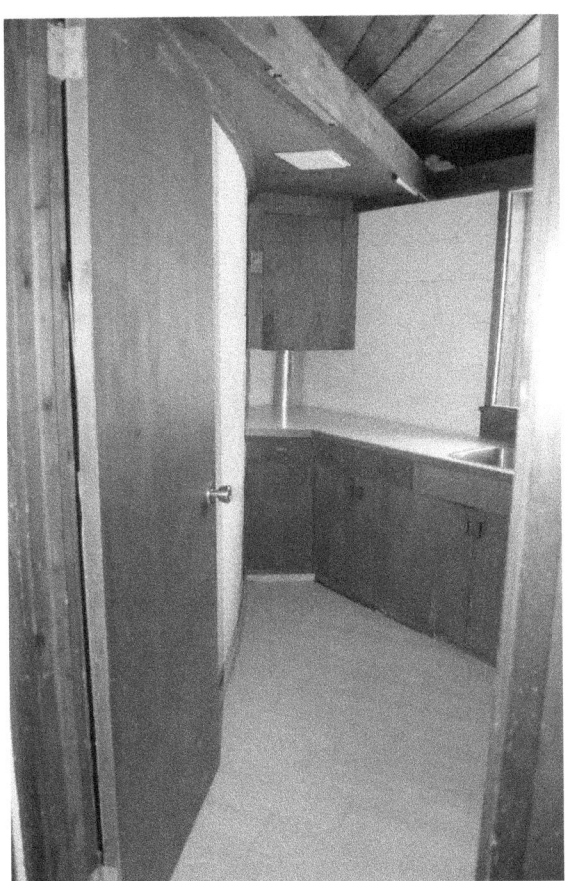

Apartment suite kitchen.
De-furnished 2017

Finishing

In the G house all interior walls (except the concrete block walls) were finished with 4x8 1/4" plywood sheets with mahogany veneer, on 2x4 stud framing. There were 1x2 cedar baseboards throughout.

Floors were initially (1960) the unfinished concrete of the exposed main slab but this was untenable due to dust and 9"x9" vinyl composite tiles were soon laid down. The tiles were redone about 1980.

The main bathroom shower and the apartment shower were finished with 4"x4" yellow tile, and kitchen and bathroom countertops were lemon-yellow arborite with mahogany edging.

Door types; mahogany panelled bi-fold doors were installed for the bedrooms and entrance vestibule clothing closets. The kitchen, bathroom and laundry had mahogany veneer plywood shelving and cupboard doors and drawers had simple wooden V handles; all were custom made on site or nearby.

With the family moved in, within a couple of years the owner painted the interior and exterior 4"x8"x16" block walls white. These were cleaned and repainted about every ten years.

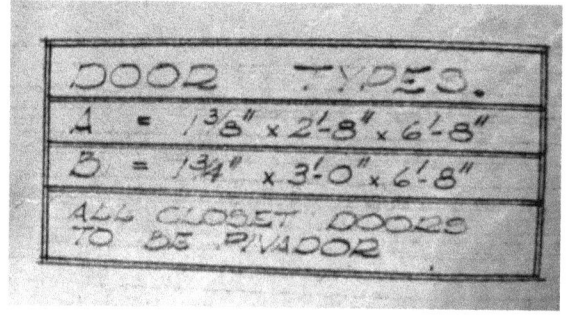

A = bedroom, bathroom and other
interior mahogany doors;
B = thicker and wider exterior
doors;
PIVADOR closet doors in entrance
vestibule and bedrooms.
(c) JWS

G house. Looking towards front door
vestibule. Construction. 1960

Looking towards recreation room.
Construction 1960

Recreation room showing stud wall
construction. 1960

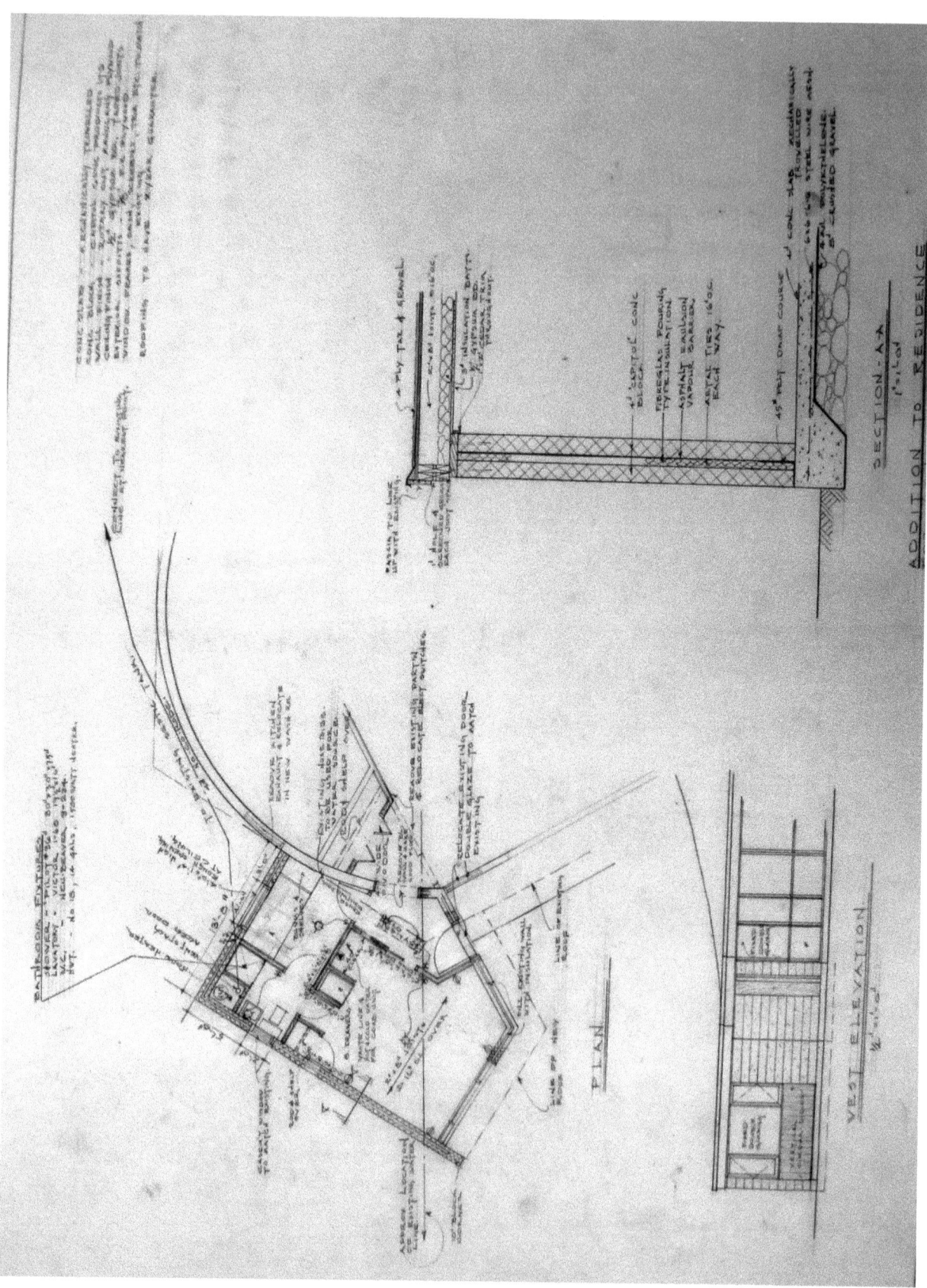

V house addition. (c) JWS

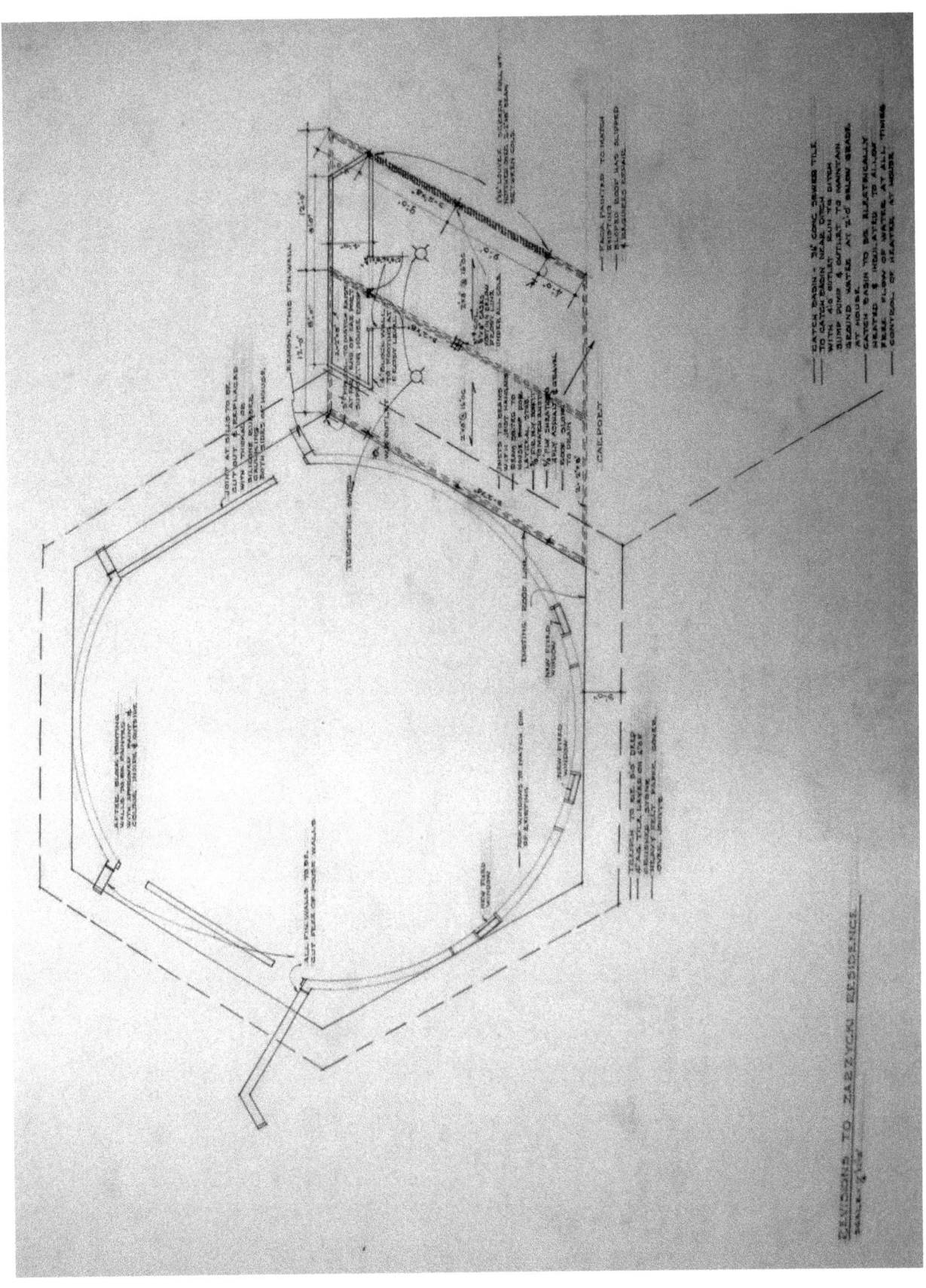

Z house addition. (c) JWS.

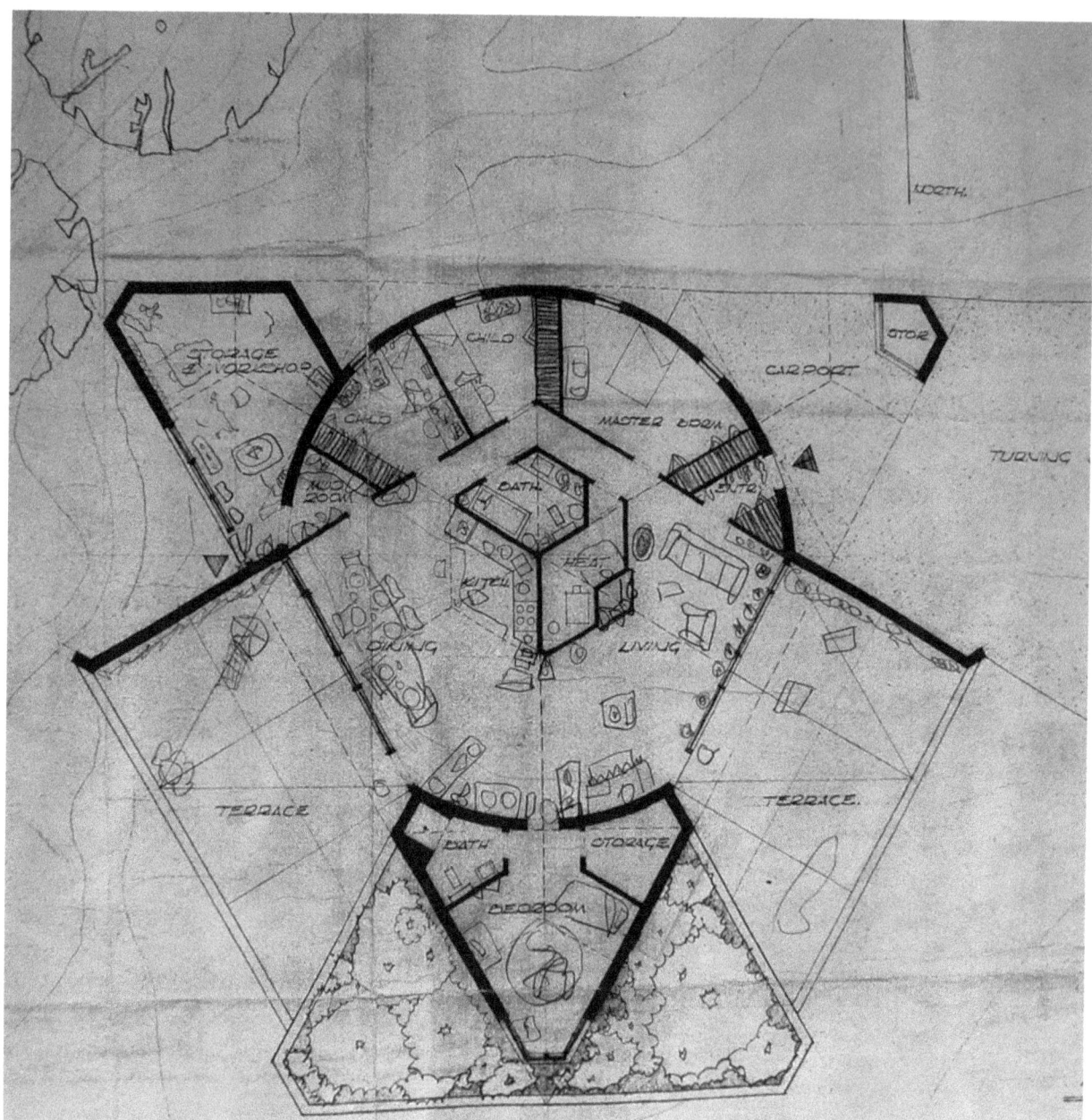

G house presentation plan with furniture drawn in. Two wing rooms and drive-through carport. Note the opposing patio windows and terraces; the ends of the privacy walls turn away from the terraces but as built they turn towards the terraces. There is one patio door aside each of the patio windows but as built there are two; the apartment wing dimensions are a bit different as built. The landscaping is idealized. (c) JWS 1959

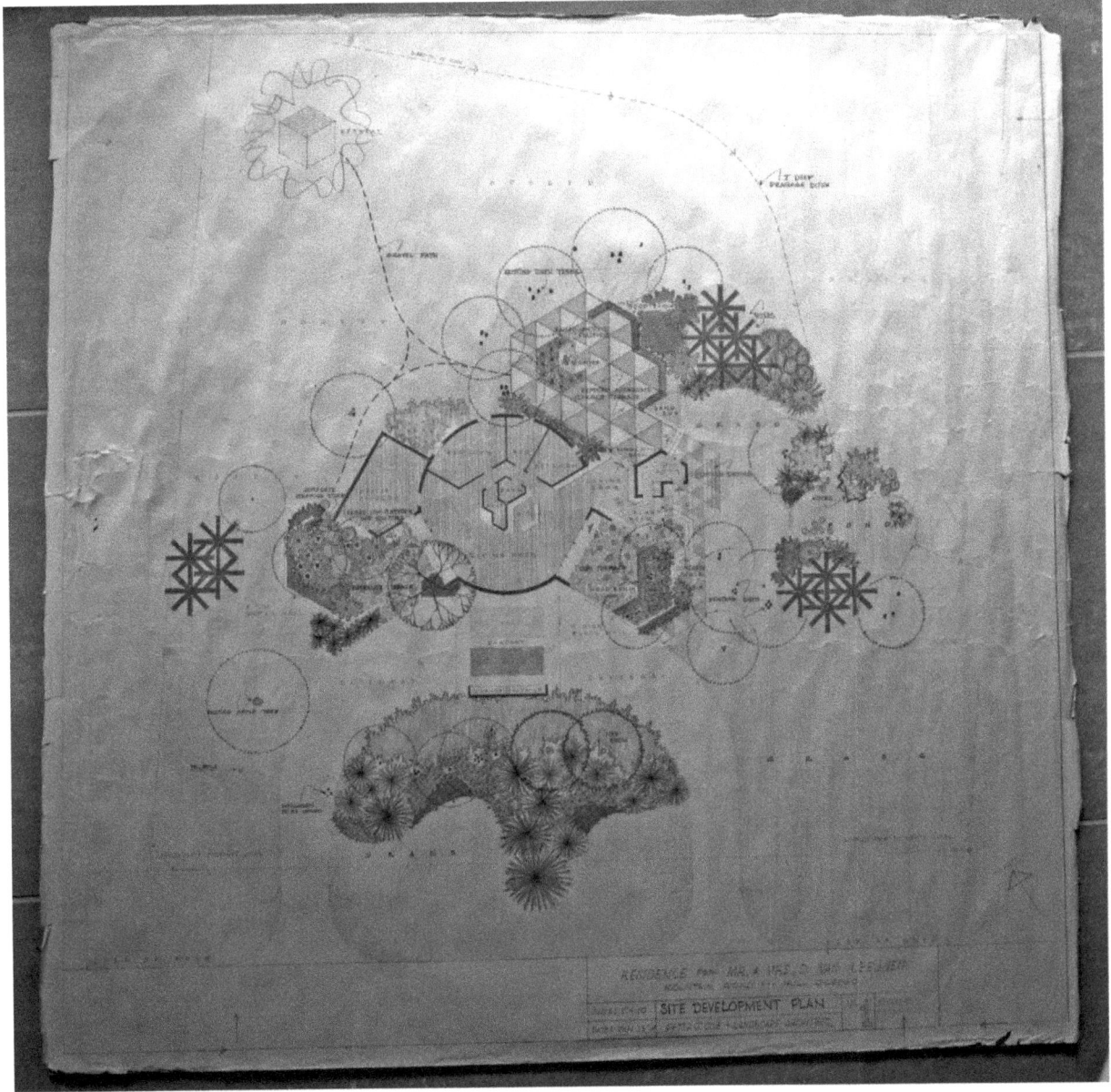

V house landscape plan of Peter Coe, 1964, coloured by J.V.
Note later rectangular room addition on left.

Living-dining. Above: looking out from central core.
Below: looking towards central core. c. 2012

Living

The photographs on these pages show further details of the architecture of the G house along with living circumstances.

Main kitchen, with P.
1960

Main kitchen, with P.
1960

Living area with P,A,B,P.
Note double doors to
apartment wing. 1960

Curved living room wall
showing roof, with P,P.
1960

Living area at interior
block wall, with D. 1960

Fireplace, with P,D,B.
1962

Protective cover. 1959

Chimney construction, with B,P. 1960

Moving day April 1960

Construction worker 1960.

Slab, with A,D,T. Note row 1 of 10 of curved concrete block wall in foreground. 1959

V house roof supports, with P. 1961

Fireplace construction, with P. 1960

At front door, with P,A. 1959

East patio windows, and roof, with B,A. 1960

Apartment exterior door and windows, with T,A. 1960

West patio, with P,G.
1960

View from apaartment
wing to living. c. 1961

Dining area and west
patio windows, with
P,?,A,B. c. 1962

West patio windows,
with P,B. c. 1978

East elevation, with
A,G. 1960

Carport. Note icicles
forming due to melt
from main roof. 1963

West patio windows and
east windows in back-
ground, with A. c. 1968

Floor & fireplace, with
B. c. 1990

South elevation, with G.
1960

East patio showing
privacy wall, with B,P.
c 1965

East elevation, with
S,P. c. 1980

Living-dining, lighting.
2011

Related Projects

These are some of the graphics related to round house concepts in the files in the National Archives Strutt collection (*Single-family Dwellings*).

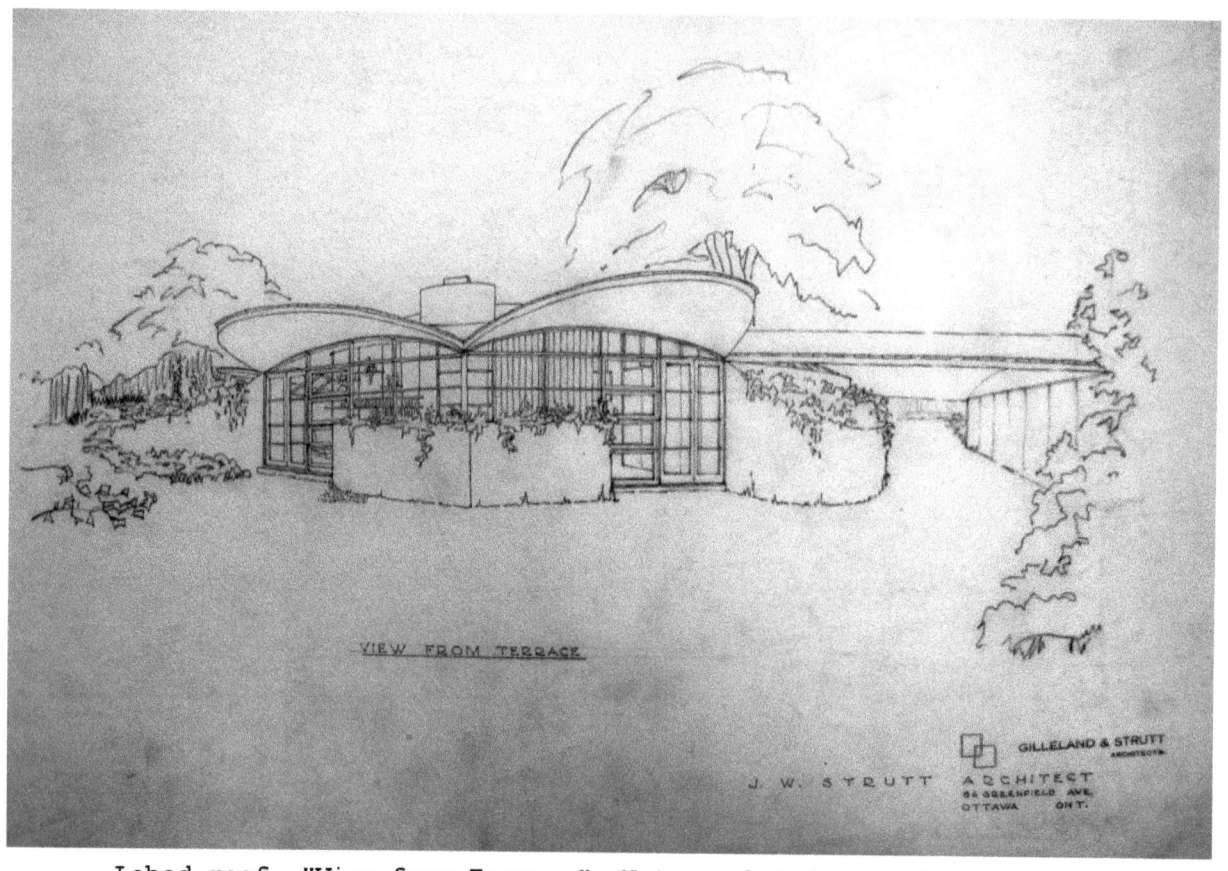

Lobed roof. "View from Terrace". Notes: abutting patio windows; carport on right. (c) JWS

Lobed roof, "View from street without carport". (c) JWS

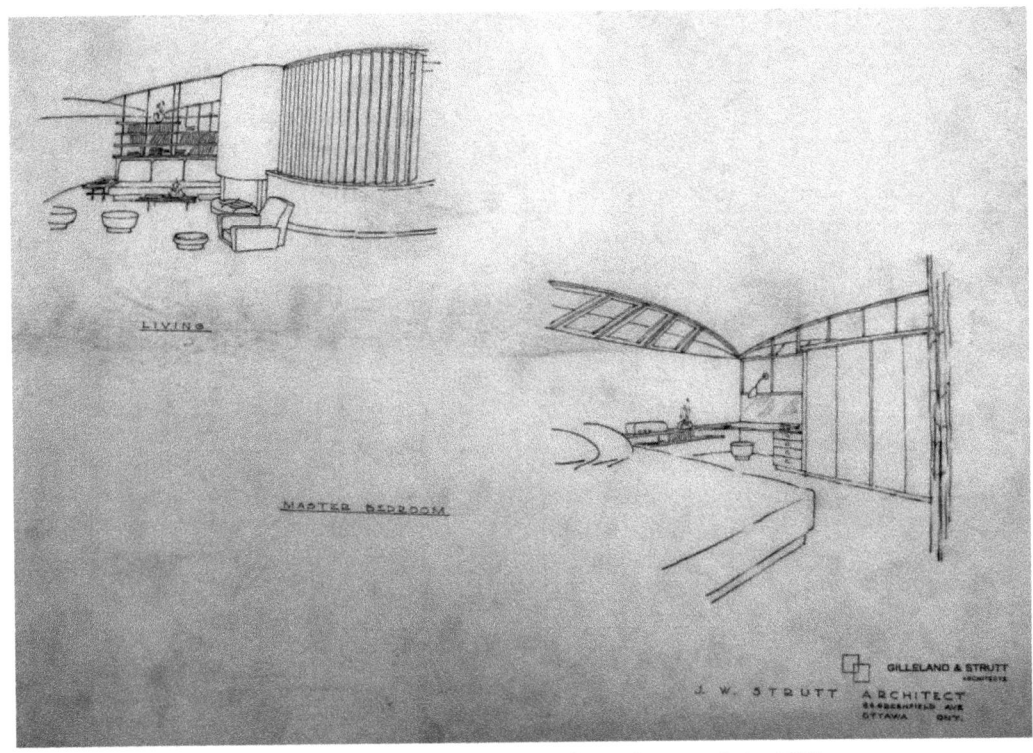

Lobed roof, interior sketches. (c) JWS

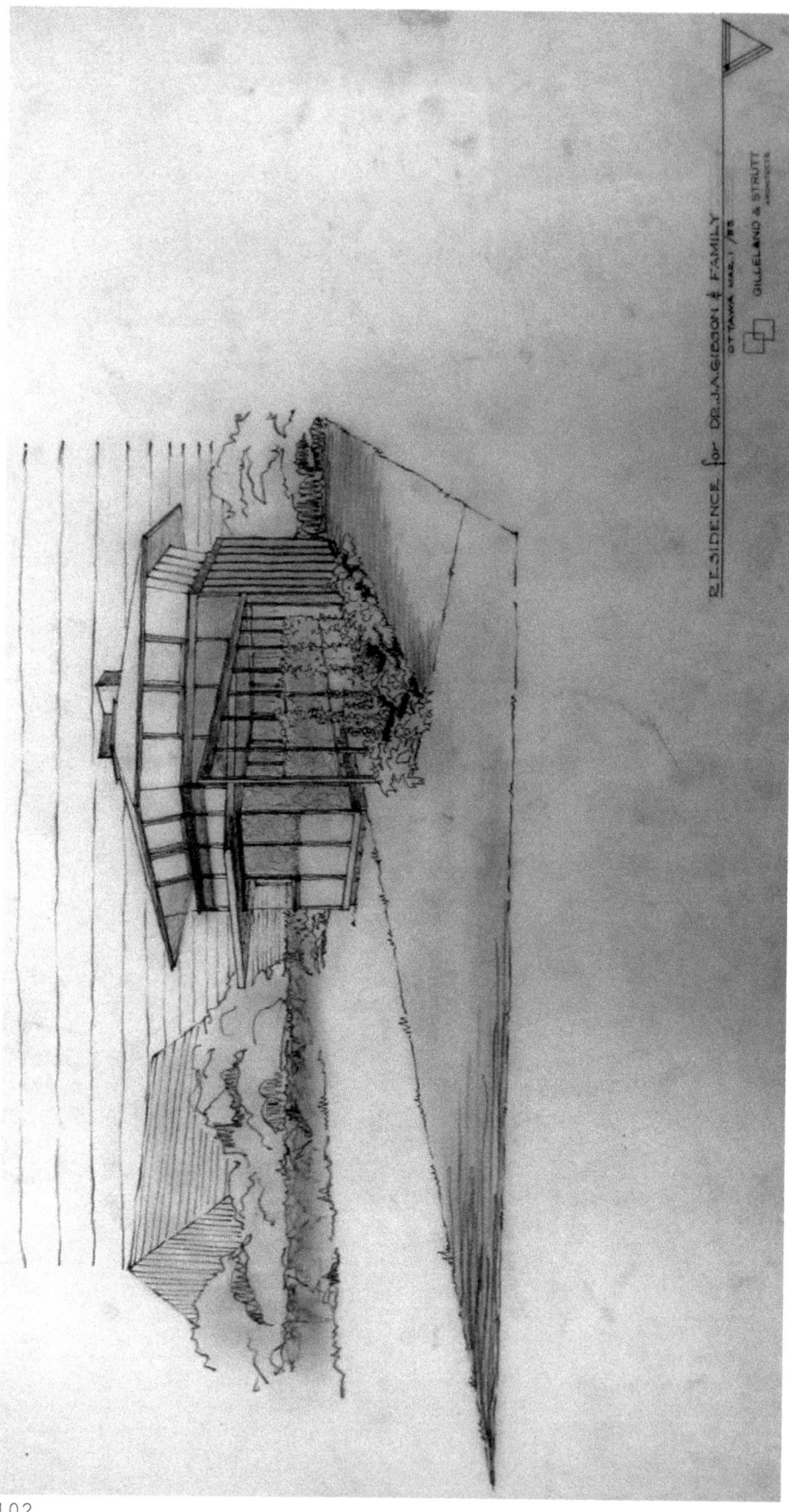

Gibson house perspective elevation. (c) JWS 1955

Facing page: Gibson house elevations. Note "Detail of continuous duct" from Plan, (insert), a concept similar to the embedded ducts in the round houses. (c) JWS 1955

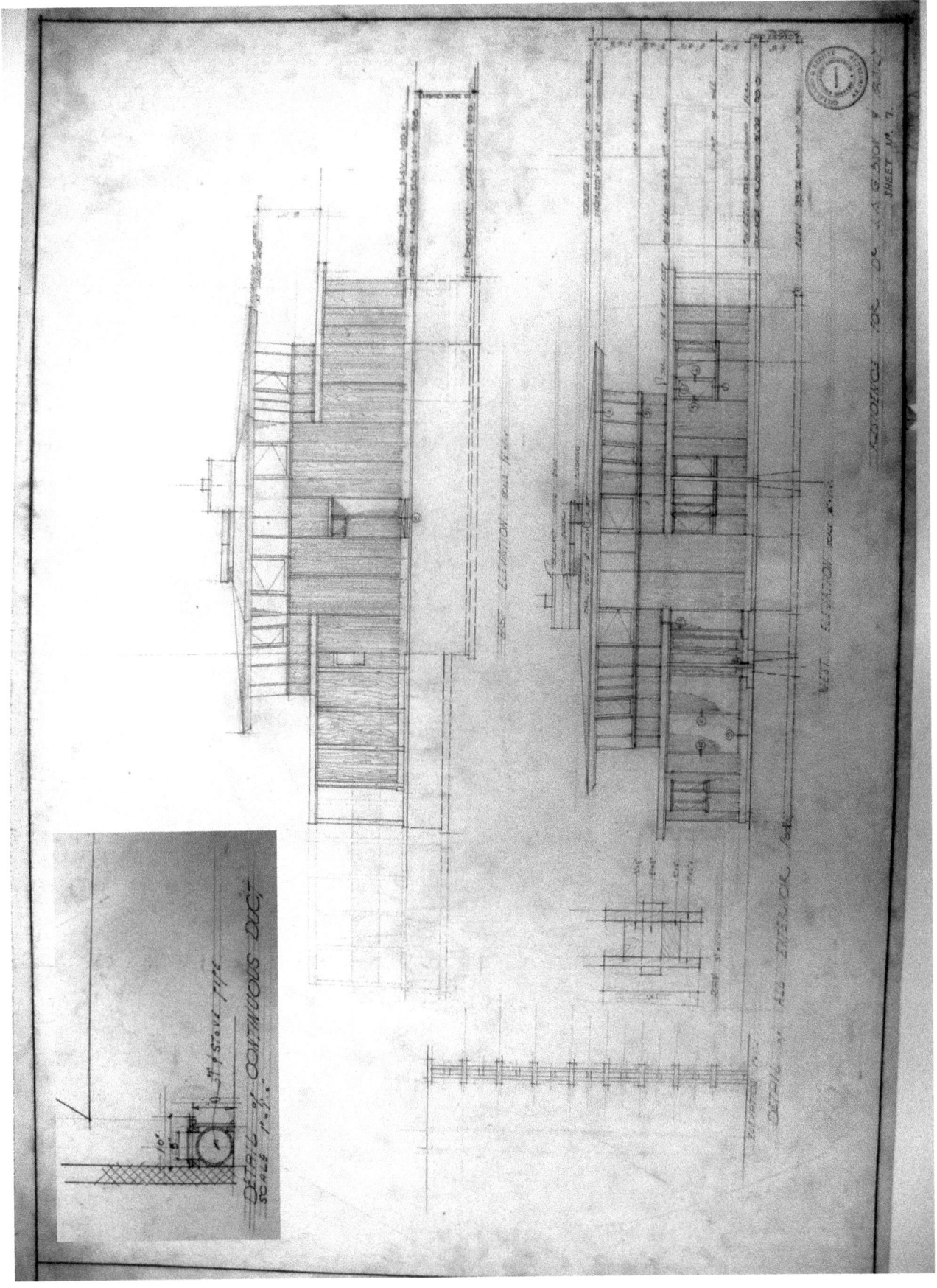

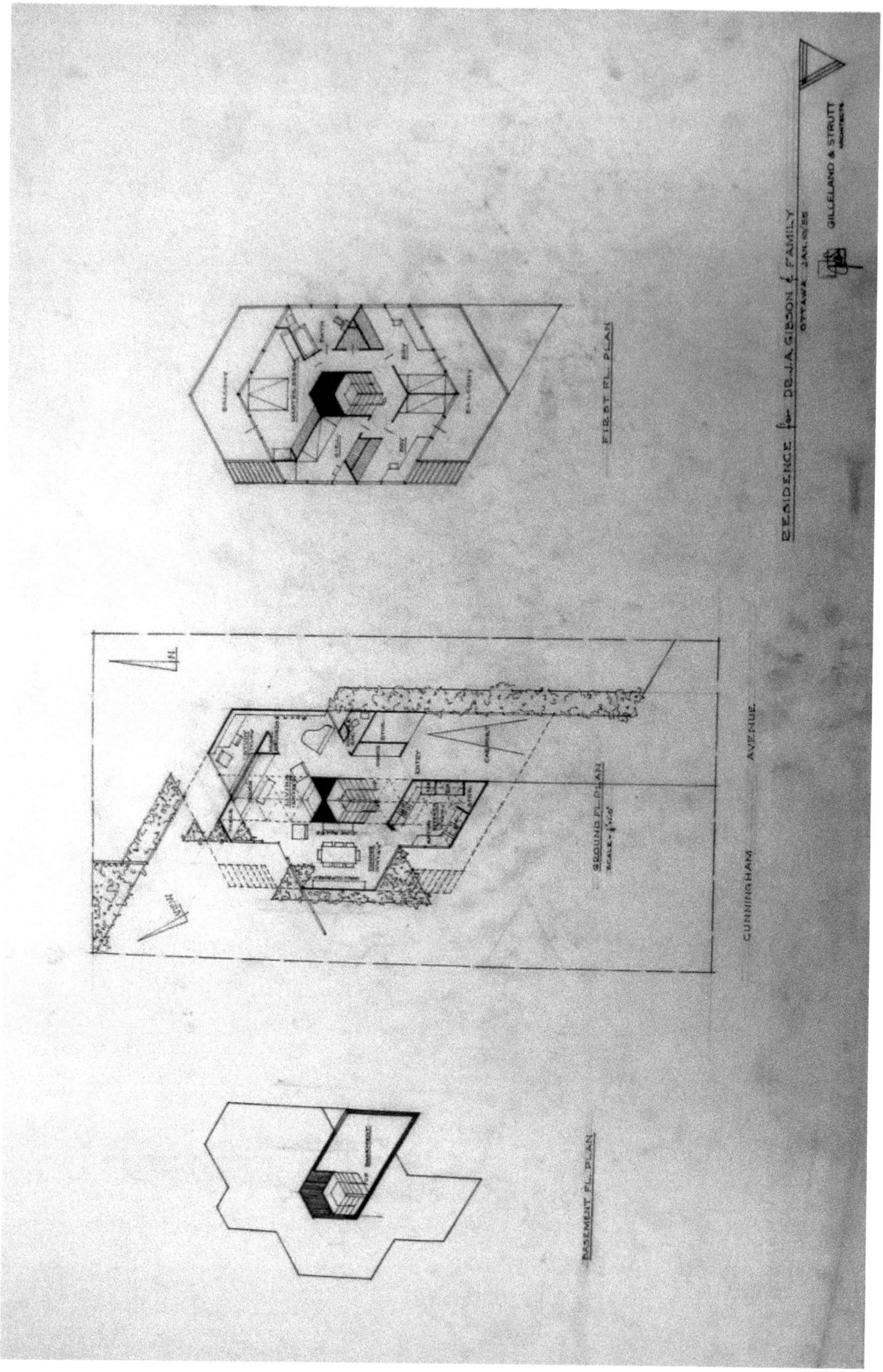

RESIDENCE for DR. J.A. GIBSON & FAMILY
OTTAWA JAN 10/59

GILLELAND & STRUTT
ARCHITECTS

FIRST FL. PLAN

GROUND FL. PLAN
SCALE ¼"=1'0"

CUNNINGHAM AVENUE

BASEMENT FL. PLAN

Gibson house floor plans. (c) JWS

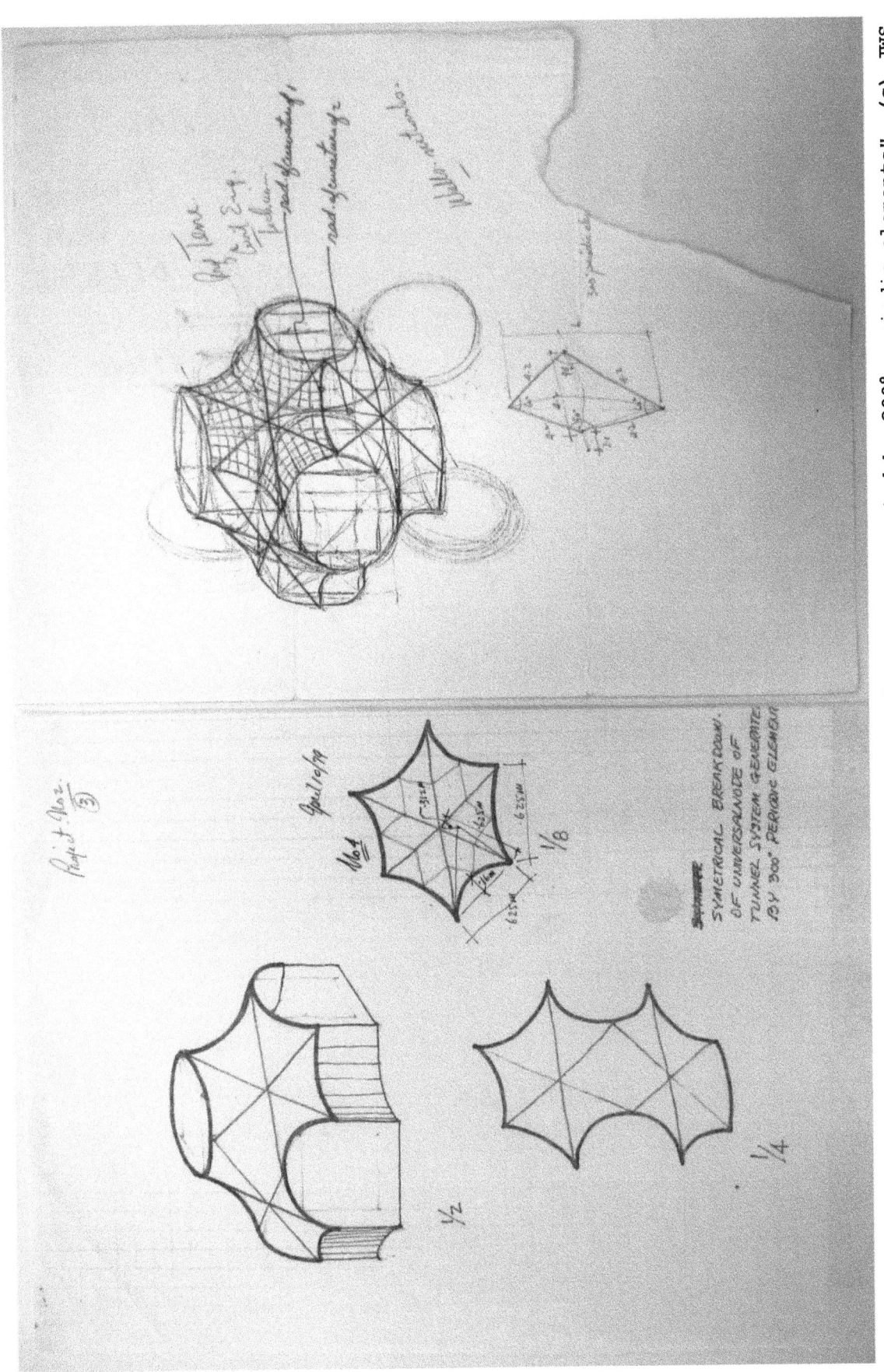

"Symetrical [sic] breakdown of universalnode of tunnel system generated by 300° periodic elements". (c) JWS

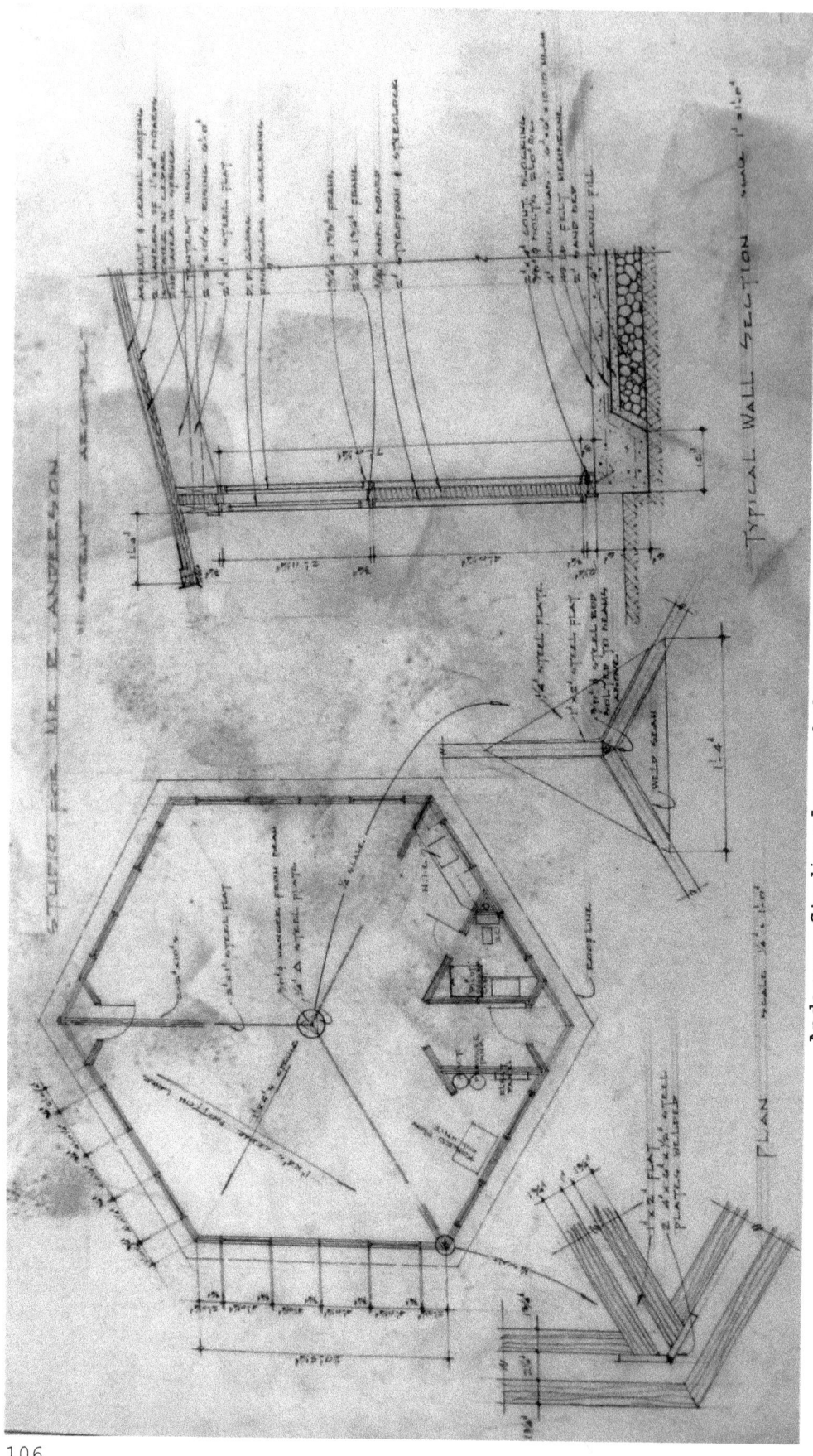

Anderson Studio plan and details c. 1970 (c) JWS

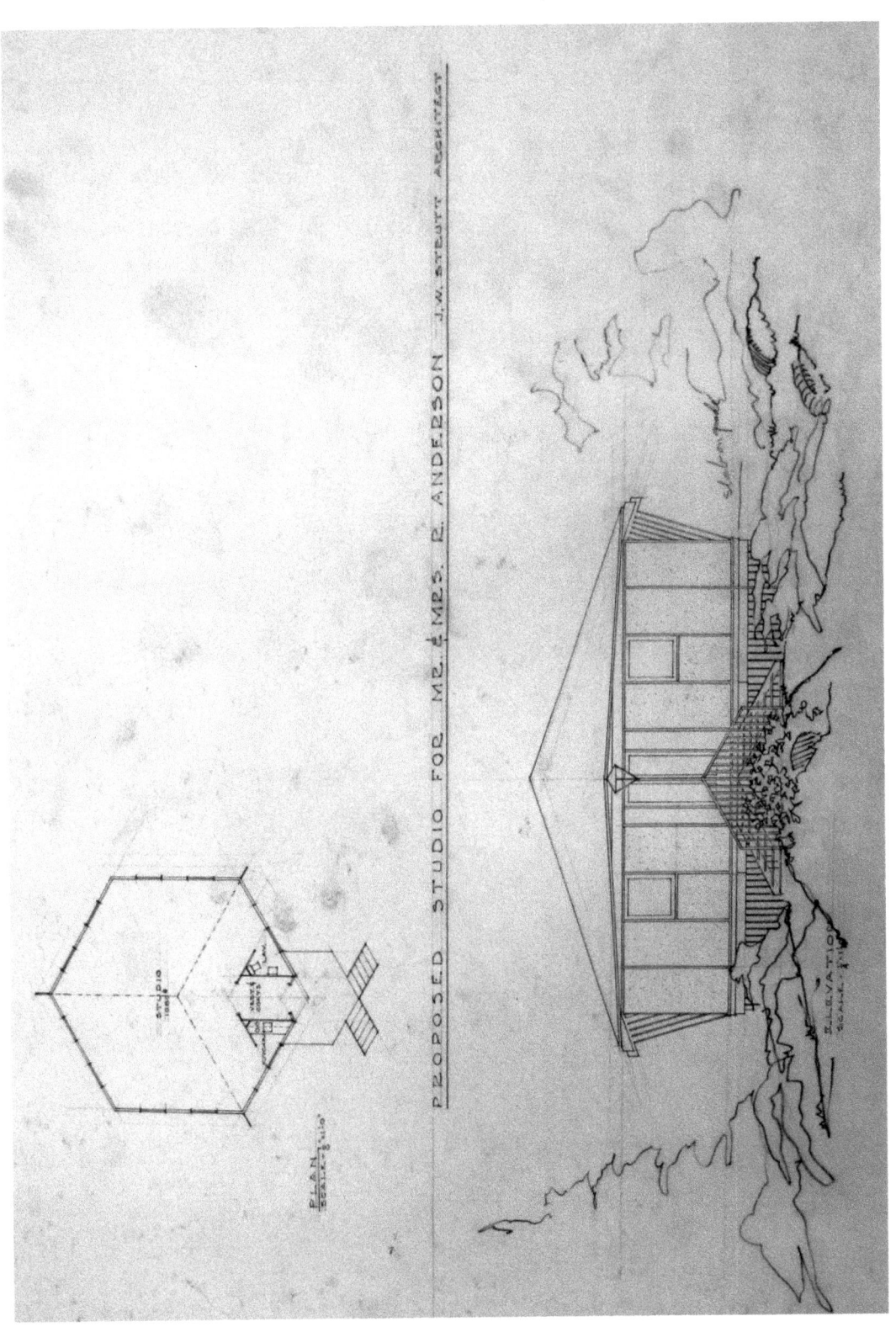

Anderson Studio plan and elevation c. 1970 (c) JWS

Bormann house perspective (c) JWS 1968

Bormann house elevation (c) JWS 1968

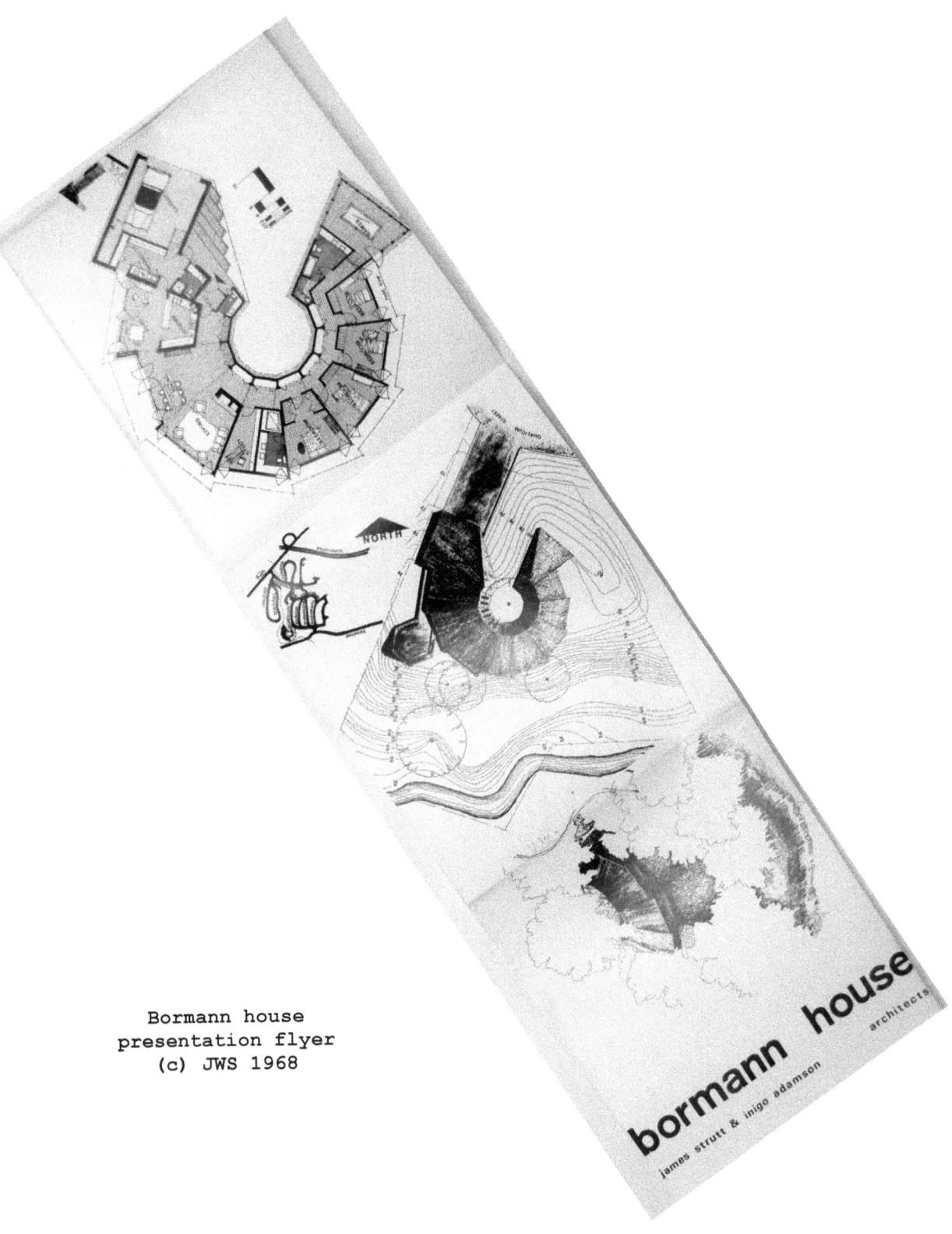

Bormann house
presentation flyer
(c) JWS 1968

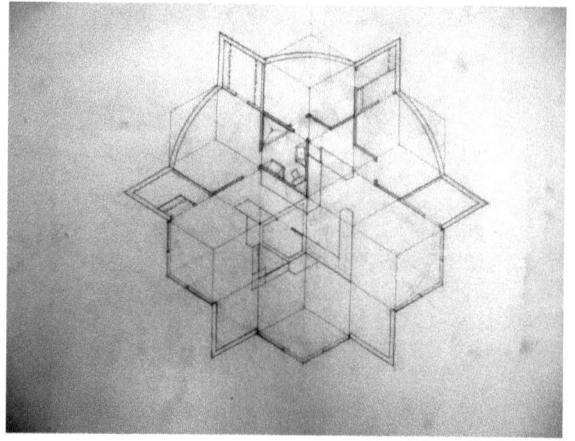

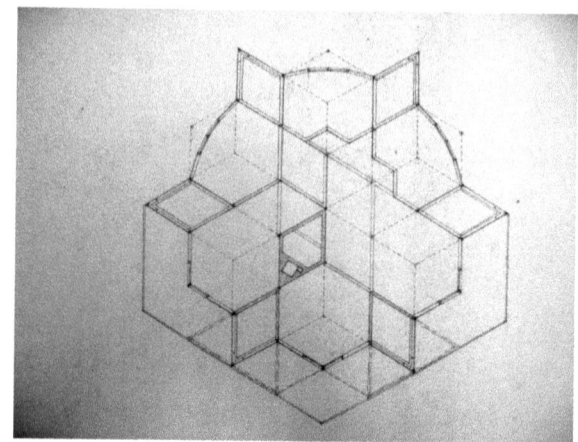

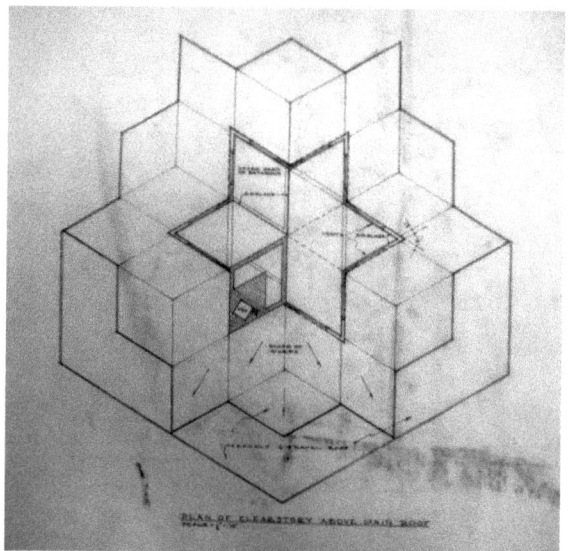

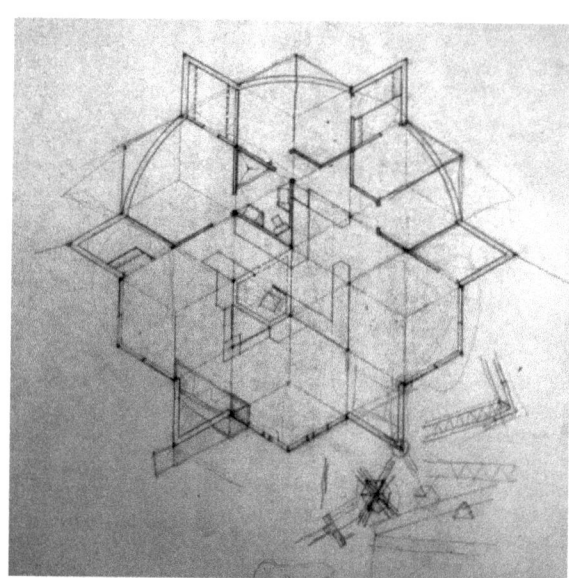

Pointed configuration
"Plan of clearstory [clerestory]
above main roof". (c) JWS

Pointed configuration. (c) JWS

Rebuild

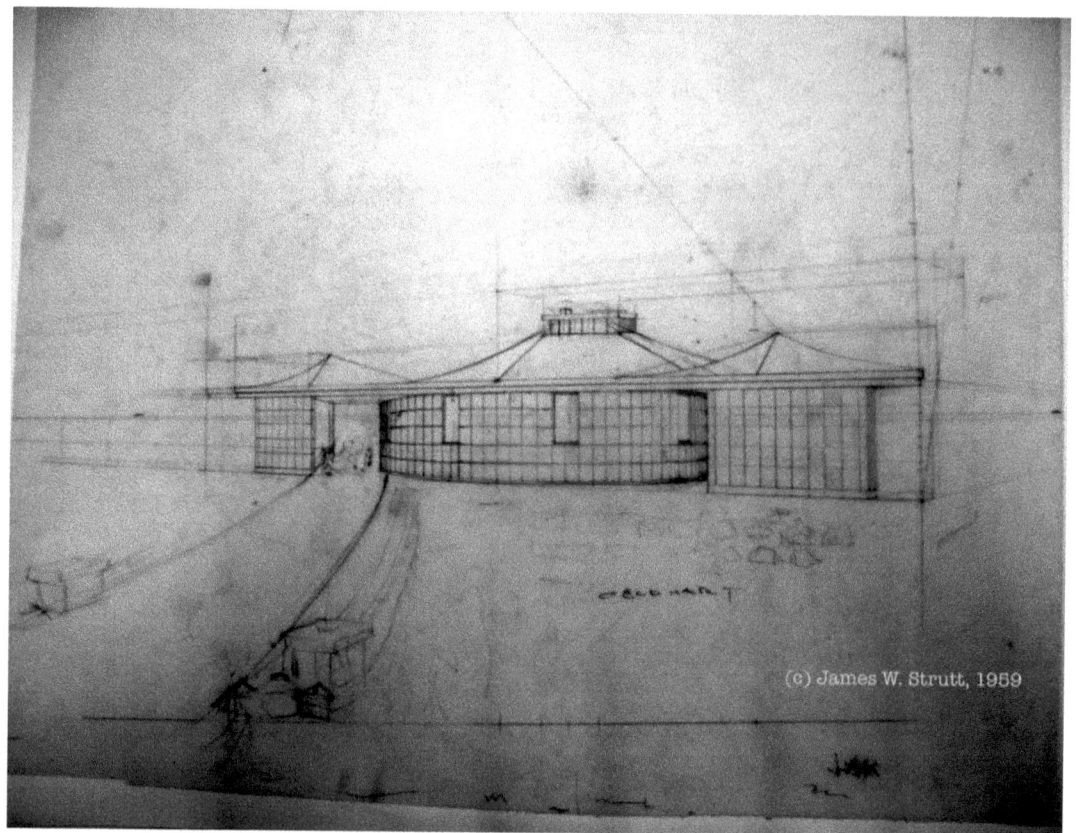

G house rear view, presentation sketch (c) JWS

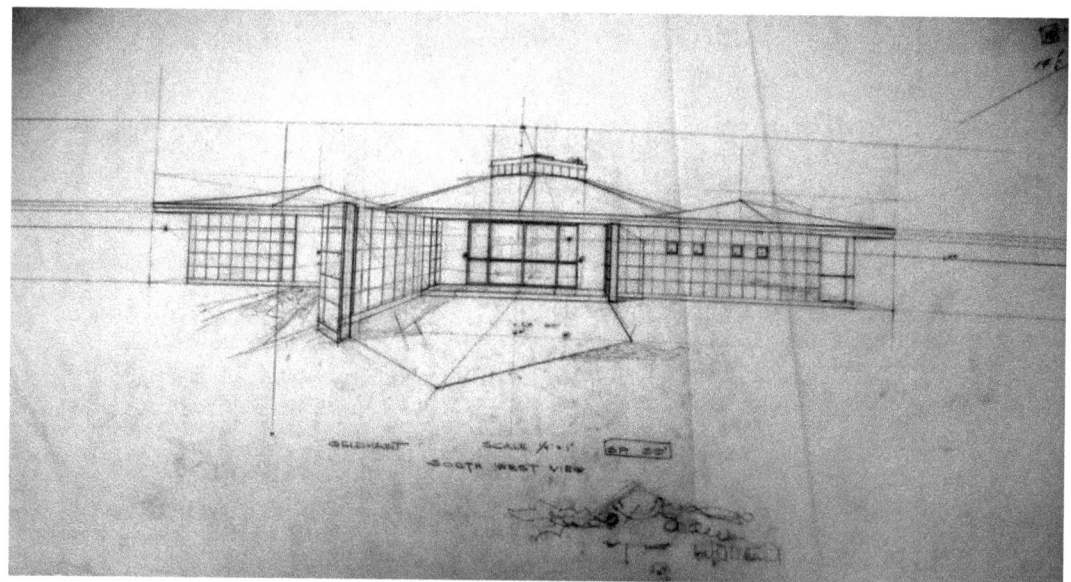

G house west side, presentation sketch (c) JWS

If the goal is to build a Strutt round house to modern standards using current techniques, that is, after six decades there being a greater awareness of the integrity of the building envelope, it is important to retain the original design and finishing. Structurally he had complied with practices at the time. However, in a climate with severe winters improvements could be made to handle cold and snow load.

(1) Foundation

Water supply and wastewater pipes (PVC) embedded in the concrete slab must be robust so as not to need servicing for the life of the building.

The concrete slab must be sitting on two layers of 2" rigid extruded foam and 12" of compacted 0-3/4" granular. At the exterior two layers extend downwards away from the building at 45° as deep as local frost penetration, to code. The slab will enclose Hydraulic Radiant Heating (HRH) which will replace the forced-air furnace and the embedded heating supply ducts. The floor will be finished, polished and sealed. The full extent of the concrete slab is an equilateral triangle of 70' sides (less a gravelled carport).

(2) HVAC

HRH replaces the forced air furnace system and there will be central air conditioning.

(3) Block Walls

Standard 4x8x16 cement blocks are used for the exterior walls sitting on the floating slab (two courses, 10 rows) with a 2" cavity filled with urethane insulation. The privacy walls and new short buttress walls are two courses on a footing capped with 2x10 cedar, insulation optional. The central hexagon is one course 20 rows with dovetailed corners at 120°. The wing rooms interior common walls are one course, 10 rows.

These block walls have a rough finish and the exterior will have mesh, insulation sheets and acrylic stucco. The interior will be finished with a sealer and paint (colour to suit).

(4) Roof

Stronger attachment of roof beams at the top of the central block hexagon and at the exterior walls. Existing was two 2x8 with 3/8" steel plate between, bolted, and 1/4" angled plates bolted to the block wall. However, in another detail drawing there was no steel plate between the beams, and the support angles were 5/8" steel.

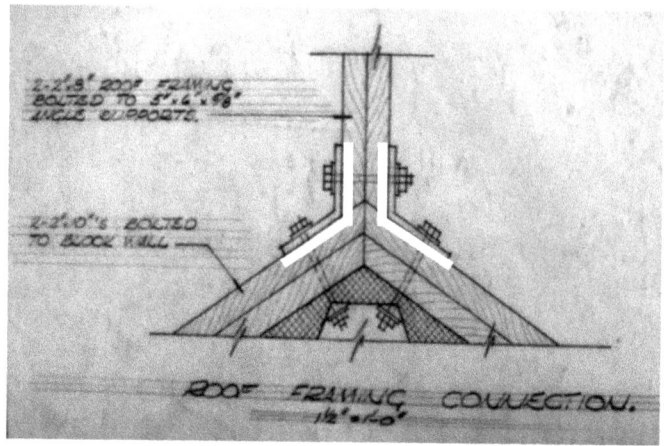

G house detail of roof beam connection at the corner of the central block hexagon. Note 5/8" angle supports and no steel plate between beams. To be reinforced. Author markup (white). Drawing (c) JWS

Stronger attachment of roof beams in the wing rooms and carport at the apex and at the exterior walls.

Short buttress block walls at the outsides of the three wings and at the rear bedrooms wall, coinciding with the location of roof beams. These are constructed in the same manner as the existing short privacy walls at the patios: ten rows of 4x8x16 blocks, two courses on a footing, with 2x10 cedar cap and front.

(5) Windows

Sealed glass panes for all windows. Patio windows will retain the custom-milled cedar mullions. Proper weather stripping and closures on all doors and opening windows.

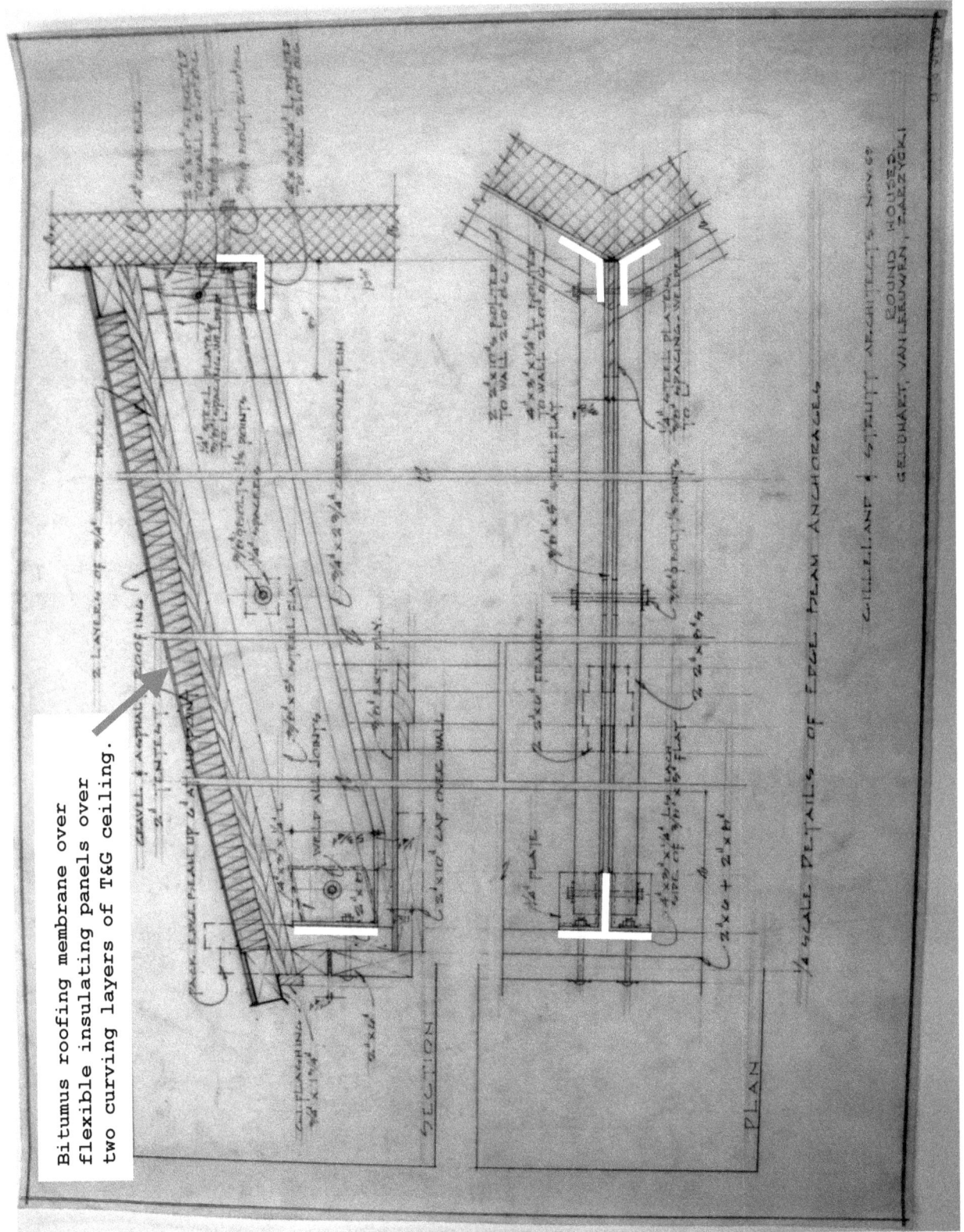

Bitumus roofing membrane over flexible insulating panels over two curving layers of T&G ceiling.

G, V and Z houses roof beam section and plan. There was a 3/8" steel plate between the two beams. White indicates areas that need to be strengthened. Author's markup. Drawing (c) JWS

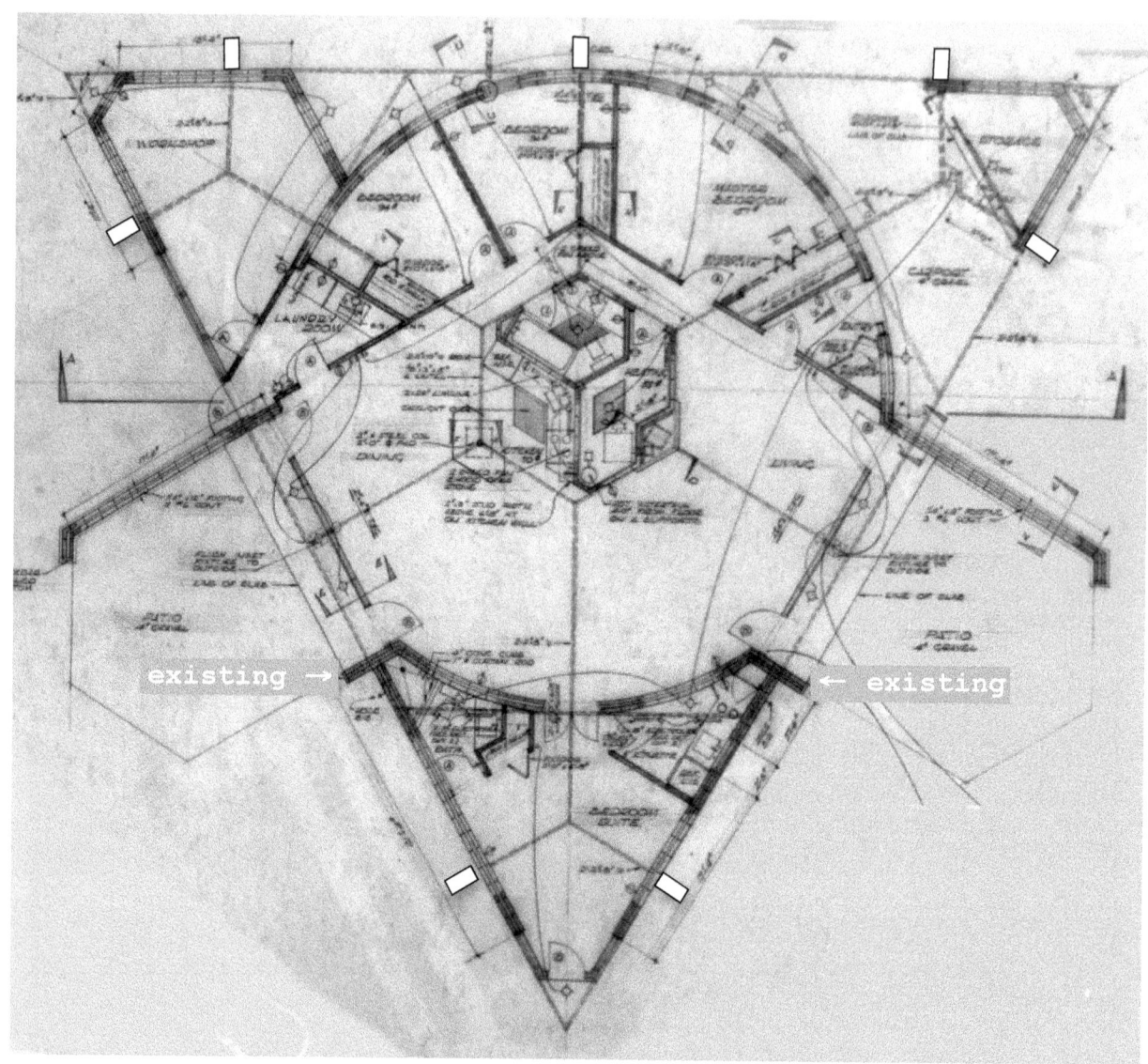

G house rebuild. Proposed short buttress block walls (white).
Author's markup; drawing (c) JWS

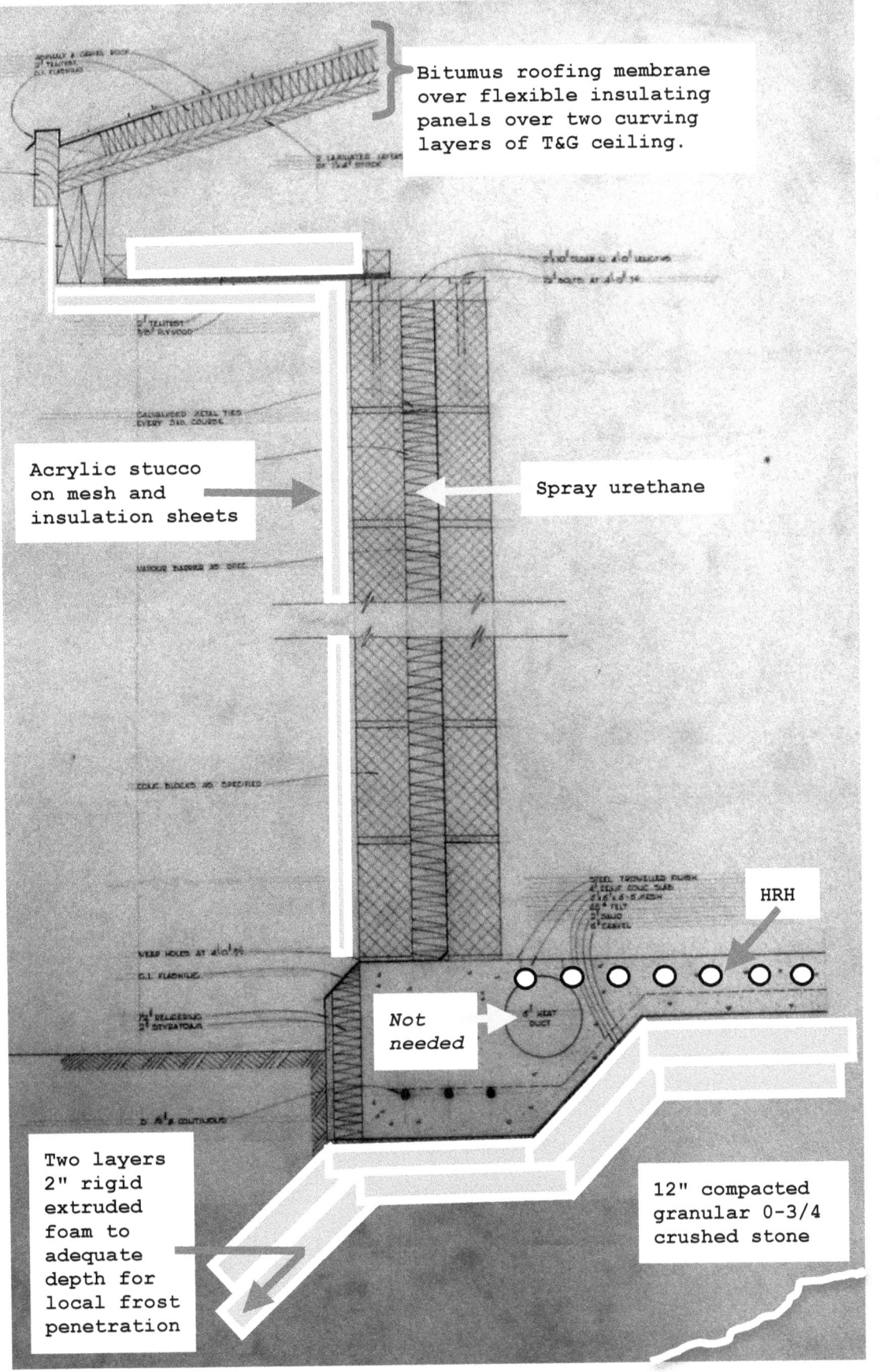

Bitumus roofing membrane over flexible insulating panels over two curving layers of T&G ceiling.

Acrylic stucco on mesh and insulation sheets

Spray urethane

HRH

Not needed

Two layers 2" rigid extruded foam to adequate depth for local frost penetration

12" compacted granular 0-3/4 crushed stone

Round houses typical exterior wall section with 4x8x16 cement blocks. Author's markup (white) showing additional insulation. Forced air heating supply ducts not needed. Interior blocks will have sealer, paint, and concrete floor will be polished and sealed. Drawing (c) JWS 1959

Location

A minimum of one acre about half of which should be on flat grade to accommodate the 70' equilateral triangular footprint of the house plus the well and septic field. The location could be in the vicinity of Strutt's own original family house north of Ottawa, Canada, in the Gatineau Park, or at Carleton University where he was director of the School of Architecture.

In a temperate climate such as the southern US it could be associated with the works of Buckminster Fuller, Soleri, Wright and other mid-century architects.

A micro house

On less-than-level terrain the wing rooms may not be possible nor necessary and the remaining circular house would be about 45' in diameter, about 1000 sq. ft. of living space. A parking carport could be located nearby and the well and septic system built as needed.

Planning and Construction

A team of architecture students with professional assistance can be formed to do the building with engineer- and architect-certified drawings. Permits and other matters would have to be handled.

Peter Geldart worked with Johns at Teron, and in other architectural firms in the Ottawa, Canada area. He grew up in a Strutt round house and later maintained and managed it. geldartp@gmail.com